THE NORTON MIX:
SOCIOLOGY

This text may contain material from *You May Ask Yourself* and/or *Essentials of Sociology*. The online StudySpace sites for these books are free and open, however you will need these registration codes to access the copyrighted streaming video in the DVD exercises:

URL: wwnorton.com/studyspace
You May Ask Yourself password: MOBI-LITY
Essentials of Sociology password: SOCI-ESSE

GENERAL EDITORS

Nathan Palmer
COORDINATING EDITOR
Georgia Southern University

Tanya Gladney
University of St. Thomas

Erica Hunter
State University of New York–Albany

Fernando I. Rivera
University of Central Florida

THE NORTON MIX:
SOCIOLOGY

A CUSTOM TEXTBOOK AND READER

Sociology 1 Reader

Professor Camelot

Saddleback College

NORTON
CUSTOM
W. W. NORTON & COMPANY, INC.
NEW YORK • LONDON

W. W. NORTON & COMPANY has been independent since its founding in 1923, when William Warder Norton and Mary D. Herter Norton first published lectures delivered at the People's Institute, the adult education division of New York City's Cooper Union. The firm soon expanded its program beyond the Institute, publishing books by celebrated academics from America and abroad. By midcentury, the two major pillars of Norton's publishing program—trade books and college texts—were firmly established. In the 1950s, the Norton family transferred control of the company to its employees, and today—with a staff of four hundred and a comparable number of trade, college, and professional titles published each year—W. W. Norton & Company stands as the largest and oldest publishing house owned wholly by its employees.

Editor: Karl Bakeman
Custom editor: Katie Hannah
Project editors: Kate Feighery and Melissa Atkin
Prodution managers, College: Ashley Horna and Diana Spiegle
Custom assistant editor: Erica Wnek
Custom editorial assistants: Elizabeth Dana and Sophie Hagen
Editorial assistant: Alicia Gonzalez-Gross
Managing editor: Marian Johnson
Copyeditor: Letta Wren Page
Design director: Rubina Yeh
Book designers: Joan Greenfield, Hope Miller Goodell, and Kiss Me I'm Polish
Text permissions manager: Megan Jackson
Text permissions editor: Nancy Rodwan
Photo permissions manager: Trish Marx
Photo permissions editor: Stephanie Romeo
Composition: Westchester Publishing Services

ISBN 978-0-393-51947-1

W. W. Norton & Company, Inc., 500 Fifth Avenue, New York, N.Y. 10110
www.wwnorton.com
W. W. Norton & Company Ltd., Castle House, 75/76 Wells Street, London W1T 3QT

CONTENTS

PETER L. BERGER

Sociology as an Individual Pastime

ociology is often misunderstood. Perhaps you are taking a sociology course because your sociology instructor had a good rating on rate-myprofessor.com, perhaps you had friends who recommended the course, or maybe the course was just scheduled in a favorable time slot. You may not have known that sociologists are known for their contributions to prison reform, school integration, and urban development. In this mid-twentieth-century article Peter Berger lays out what sociology is all about and the motivations that drive sociological work. If you ever wondered how **society** functions, sociology will give you the tools to find out.

IT IS GRATIFYING FROM CERTAIN VALUE POSITIONS (INCLUDING some of this writer's) that sociological insights have served in a number of instances to improve the lot of groups of human beings by uncovering morally shocking conditions or by clearing away collective illusions or by showing that socially desired results could be obtained in more humane fashion. One might point, for example, to some applications of sociological knowledge in the penological practice of Western countries. Or one might cite the use made of sociological studies in the Supreme Court decision of 1954 on racial segregation in the public schools. Or one could look at the applications of other sociological studies to the humane planning of urban redevelopment. Certainly the sociologist who is morally and politically sensitive will derive gratification from such instances. But, once more, it will be well to keep in mind that what is at issue here is not sociological understanding as such but certain applications of this understanding. It is not difficult to see how the same understanding could be applied with opposite intentions. Thus the sociological understanding of the dynamics of racial prejudice can be applied effectively by those promoting intragroup hatred as well as by those wanting to spread tolerance. And the sociological understanding of the nature of human solidarity can be employed in the service of both totalitarian and democratic regimes.

* * *

One [more recent] image [of the sociologist is that of] a gatherer of statistics about human behavior. The sociologist is here seen essentially as an aide-de-camp to an IBM machine. He goes out with a questionnaire, interviews people selected at random, then goes home, enters his tabulations onto innumerable punch cards, which are then fed into a machine. In all of this, of course, he is supported by a large staff and a very large budget. Included in this image is the implication that the results of all this effort are picayune, a pedantic re-statement of what everybody knows anyway. As one observer remarked pithily, a sociologist is a fellow who spends $100,000 to find his way to a house of ill repute.[1]

This image of the sociologist has been strengthened in the public mind by the activities of many agencies that might well be called parasociological, mainly agencies concerned with public opinion and market trends. The pollster has become a well-known figure in American life, importuning people about their views from foreign policy to toilet paper. Since the methods used in the pollster business bear close resemblance to sociological research, the growth of this image of the sociologist is understandable. The Kinsey studies of American sexual behavior have probably greatly augmented the impact of this image. The fundamental sociological question, whether concerned with premarital petting or with Republican votes or with the incidence of gang knifings, is always presumed to be "how often?" or "how many?"

* * *

Now it must be admitted, albeit regretfully, that this image of the sociologist and his trade is not altogether a product of fantasy. Beginning shortly after World War I, American sociology turned rather resolutely away from theory to an intensive preoccupation with narrowly circumscribed empirical studies. In connection with this turn, sociologists increasingly refined their research techniques. Among these, very naturally, statistical techniques figured prominently. Since about the mid 1940s there has been a revival of interest in sociological theory, and there are good indications that this tendency away from a narrow empiricism is continuing to gather momentum. It remains true, however, that a goodly part of the sociological enterprise in this country continues to consist of little studies of obscure fragments of social life, irrelevant to any broader

---

[1] That is, a brothel.

theoretical concern. One glance at the table of contents of the major sociological journals or at the list of papers read at sociological conventions will confirm this statement.

* * *

Statistical data by themselves do not make sociology. They become sociology only when they are sociologically interpreted, put within a theoretical frame of reference that is sociological. Simple counting, or even correlating different items that one counts, is not sociology. There is almost no sociology in the Kinsey reports. This does not mean that the data in these studies are not true or that they cannot be relevant to sociological understanding. They are, taken by themselves, raw materials that can be used in sociological interpretation. The interpretation, however, must be broader than the data themselves. So the sociologist cannot arrest himself at the frequency tables of premarital petting or extramarital pederasty. These enumerations are meaningful to him only in terms of their much broader implications for an understanding of institutions and values in our society. To arrive at such understanding the sociologist will often have to apply statistical techniques, especially when he is dealing with the mass phenomena of modern social life. But sociology consists of statistics as little as philology consists of conjugating irregular verbs or chemistry of making nasty smells in test tubes.

Sociology has, from its beginnings, understood itself as a science. There has been much controversy about the precise meaning of this self-definition. * * * But the allegiance of sociologists to the scientific ethos has meant everywhere a willingness to be bound by certain scientific canons of procedure. If the sociologist remains faithful to his calling, his statements must be arrived at through the observation of certain rules of evidence that allow others to check on or to repeat or to develop his findings further. It is this scientific discipline that often supplies the motive for reading a sociological work as against, say, a novel on the same topic that might describe matters in much more impressive and convincing language. As sociologists tried to develop their scientific rules of evidence, they were compelled to reflect upon methodological problems. This is why methodology is a necessary and valid part of the sociological enterprise.

At the same time it is quite true that some sociologists, especially in America, have become so preoccupied with methodological questions that they have ceased to be interested in society at all. As a result, they have found out nothing of significance about any aspect of social life, since in science as in love a concentration on technique is quite likely to lead to impotence. Much of this fixation on methodology can be explained in terms of the urge of a relatively new discipline to find acceptance on the academic scene. Since science is an almost sacred entity among Americans in general and American academicians in particular, the desire to emulate the procedures of the older natural sciences is very strong among the newcomers in the marketplace of erudition.

* * *

As they become more secure in their academic status, it may be expected that this methodological inferiority complex will diminish even further.

The charge that many sociologists write in a barbaric dialect must also be admitted with similar reservations. Any scientific discipline must develop a terminology. This is self-evident for a discipline such as, say, nuclear physics that deals with matters unknown to most people and for which no words exist in common speech. However, terminology is possibly even more important for the social sciences, just because their subject matter *is* familiar and just because words *do* exist to denote it. Because we are well acquainted with the social institutions that surround us, our perception of them is imprecise and often erroneous. In very much the same way most of us will have considerable difficulty giving an accurate description of our parents, husbands or wives, children or close friends. Also, our language is often (and perhaps blessedly) vague and confusing in its references to social reality. Take for an example the concept of *class*, a very important one in sociology. There must be dozens of meanings that this term may have in common speech—income brackets, races, ethnic groups, power cliques, intelligence ratings, and many others. It is obvious that the sociologist must have a precise, unambiguous definition of the concept if his work is to proceed with any degree of scientific rigor. In view of these facts, one can understand that some sociologists have been tempted to invent altogether new words to avoid the semantic traps of the vernacular usage.

Finally, we would look at an image of the sociologist not so much in his professional role as in his being, supposedly, a certain kind of person. This is the image of the sociologist as a detached, sardonic observer, and a cold manipulator of men. Where this image prevails, it may represent an ironic triumph of the sociologist's own efforts to be accepted as a genuine scientist. The sociologist here becomes the self-appointed superior man, standing off from the warm vitality of common existence, finding his satisfactions not in living but in coolly appraising the lives of others, filing them away in little categories, and thus presumably missing the real significance of what he is observing. Further, there is the notion that, when he involves himself in social processes at all, the sociologist does so as an uncommitted technician, putting his manipulative skills at the disposal of the powers that be.

This last image is probably not very widely held. * * * As a general portrait of the contemporary sociologist it is certainly a gross distortion. It fits very few individuals that anyone is likely to meet in this country today. The problem of the political role of the social scientist is, nevertheless, a very genuine one. For instance, the employment of sociologists by certain branches of industry and government raises moral questions that ought to be faced more widely than they have been so far. These are, however, moral questions that concern all men in positions of responsibility in modern society. The image of the sociologist as an observer without compassion and a manipulator without conscience need not detain us further here. * * * As for contemporary sociologists, most of them would lack the emotional equipment for such a role, even if they should aspire to it in moments of feverish fantasy.

How then are we to conceive of the sociologist? In discussing the various images of him that abound in the popular mind we have already brought out certain elements that would have to go into our conception.

* * *

The sociologist, then, is someone concerned with understanding society in a disciplined way. The nature of this discipline is scientific. This means that what the sociologist finds and says about the social phenomena he studies occurs within a certain rather strictly defined frame of reference. One of the main characteristics of this scientific frame of reference is that operations are bound by certain rules of evidence. As a scientist, the sociologist tries to be objective, to control his personal preferences and prejudices, to perceive clearly rather than to judge normatively. This restraint, of course, does not embrace the totality of the sociologist's existence as a human being, but is limited to his operations *qua* sociologist. Nor does the sociologist claim that his frame of reference is the only one within which society can be looked at. For that matter, very few scientists in any field would claim today that one should look at the world only scientifically. The botanist looking at a daffodil has no reason to dispute the right of the poet to look at the same object in a very different manner. There are many ways of playing. The point is not that one denies other people's games but that one is clear about the rules of one's own. The game of the sociologist, then, uses scientific rules. As a result, the sociologist must be clear in his own mind as to the meaning of these rules. That is, he must concern himself with methodological questions. Methodology does not constitute his goal. The latter, let us recall once more, is the attempt to understand society. Methodology helps in reaching this goal. In order to understand society, or that segment of it that he is studying at the moment, the sociologist will use a variety of means. Among these are statistical techniques. Statistics can be very useful in answering certain sociological questions. But statistics does not constitute sociology. As a scientist, the sociologist will have to be concerned with the exact significance of the terms he is using. That is, he will have to be careful about terminology. This does not have to mean that he must invent a new language of his own, but it does mean that he cannot naively use the language of everyday discourse. Finally, the interest of the sociologist is primarily theoretical. That is, he is interested in understanding for its own sake. He may be aware of or even concerned with the practical applicability and consequences of his findings, but at that point he leaves the sociological frame of reference as such and moves into realms of values, beliefs and ideas that he shares with other men who are not sociologists.

* * *

THE MOTIVATION TO DO SOCIOLOGY

We would like to go a little bit further here and ask a somewhat more personal (and therefore, no doubt, more controversial) question. We would like to ask not only what it is that the sociologist is doing but also what it is that drives him to it. Or, to use the phrase Max Weber used in a similar connection, we want to inquire a little into the nature of the sociologist's demon. In doing so, we shall evoke an image that is not so much ideal-typical in the above sense but more confessional in the sense of personal commitment. Again, we are not interested in excommunicating anyone. The game of sociology goes on in a spacious playground. We are just describing a little more closely those we would like to tempt to join our game.

We would say then that the sociologist (that is, the one we would really like to invite to our game) is a person intensively, endlessly, shamelessly interested in the doings of men. His natural habitat is all the human gathering places of the world, wherever men come together. The sociologist may be interested in many other things. But his consuming interest remains in the world of men, their institutions, their history, their passions. And since he is interested in men, nothing that men do can be altogether tedious for him. He will naturally be interested in the events that engage men's ultimate beliefs, their moments of tragedy and grandeur and ecstasy. But he will also be fascinated by the common place, the everyday. He will know reverence, but this reverence will not prevent him from wanting to see and to understand. He may sometimes feel revulsion or contempt. But this also will not deter him from wanting to have his questions answered. The sociologist, in his quest for understanding, moves through the world of men without respect for the usual lines of demarcation. Nobility and degradation, power and obscurity, intelligence and folly—these are equally *interesting* to him, however unequal they may be in his personal values or tastes. Thus his questions may lead him to all possible levels of society, the best and the least known places, the most respected and the most despised. And, if he is a good sociologist, he will find himself in all these places because his own questions have so taken possession of him that he has little choice but to seek for answers.

It would be possible to say the same things in a lower key. We could say that the sociologist, but for the grace of his academic title, is the man who must listen to gossip despite himself, who is tempted to look through keyholes, to read other people's mail, to open closed cabinets. Before some otherwise unoccupied psychologist sets out now to construct an aptitude test for sociologists on the basis of sublimated voyeurism, let us quickly say that we are speaking merely by way of analogy. Perhaps some little boys consumed with curiosity to watch their maiden aunts in the bathroom later become inveterate sociologists. This is quite uninteresting. What interests us is the curiosity that grips any sociologist in front of a closed door behind which there are human voices. If he is a good sociologist, he will want to open that door, to understand these voices. Behind each closed door he will anticipate some new facet of human life not yet perceived and understood.

The sociologist will occupy himself with matters that others regard as too sacred or as too distasteful for dispassionate investigation. He will find rewarding the company of priests or of prostitutes, depending not on his personal preferences but on the questions he happens to be asking at the moment. He will also concern himself with matters that others may find much too boring. He will be interested in the human interaction that goes with warfare or with great intellectual discoveries, but also in the relations between people employed in a restaurant or between a group of little girls playing with their dolls. His main focus of attention is not the ultimate significance of what men do, but the action in itself, as another example of the infinite richness of human conduct. So much for the image of our playmate.

In these journeys through the world of men the sociologist will inevitably encounter other professional Peeping Toms. Sometimes these will resent his presence, feeling that he is poaching on their preserves. In some places the sociologist will meet up with the economist, in others with the political scientist, in yet others with the psychologist or the ethnologist. Yet chances are that the questions that have brought him to these same places are different from the ones that propelled his fellow-trespassers. The sociologist's questions always remain essentially the same: "What are people doing with each other here?" "What are their relationships to each other?" "How are these relationships organized in institutions?" "What are the collective ideas that move men and institutions?" In trying to answer these questions in specific instances, the sociologist will, of course, have to deal with economic or political matters, but he will do so in a way rather different from that of the economist or the political scientist. The scene that he contemplates is the same human scene that these other scientists concern themselves with. But the sociologist's angle of vision is different. When this is understood, it becomes clear that it makes little sense to try to stake out a special enclave within which the sociologist will carry on business in his own right. * * * There is, however, one traveler whose path the sociologist will cross more often than anyone else's on his journeys. This is the historian. Indeed, as soon as the sociologist turns from the present to the past, his preoccupations are very hard indeed to distinguish from those of the historian. However, we shall leave this relationship to a later part of our considerations. Suffice it to say here that the sociological journey will be much impoverished unless it is punctuated frequently by conversation with that other particular traveler.

Any intellectual activity derives excitement from the moment it becomes a trail of discovery. In some fields of learning this is the discovery of worlds previously unthought and unthinkable. This is the excitement of the astronomer or of the nuclear physicist on the antipodal boundaries of the realities that man is capable of conceiving. But it can also be the excitement of bacteriology or geology. In a different way it can be the excitement of the linguist discovering new realms of human expression or of the anthropologist exploring human customs in faraway countries. In such discovery, when undertaken with passion, a widening of awareness, sometimes a veritable transformation of consciousness, occurs. The universe turns out to be much more wonderful than one had ever dreamed. The excitement of sociology is usually of a different sort. Sometimes, it is true, the sociologist penetrates into worlds that had previously been quite unknown to him—for instance, the world of crime, or the world of some bizarre religious sect, or the world fashioned by the exclusive concerns of some group such as medical specialists or military leaders or advertising executives. However, much of the time the sociologist moves in sectors of experience that are familiar to him and to most people in his society. He investigates communities, institutions and activities that one can read about every day in the newspapers. Yet there is another excitement of discovery beckoning in his investigations. It is not the excitement of coming upon the totally unfamiliar, but rather the excitement of finding the familiar becoming transformed in its meaning. The fascination of sociology lies in the fact that its perspective makes us see in a new light the very world in which we have lived all our lives. This also constitutes a transformation of consciousness. Moreover, this transformation is more relevant existentially than that of many other intellectual disciplines, because it is more difficult to segregate in some special compartment of the mind. The astronomer does not live in the remote galaxies, and the nuclear physicist can, outside his laboratory, eat and laugh and marry and vote without thinking about the insides of the atom. The geologist looks at rocks only at appropriate times, and the linguist speaks English with his wife. The sociologist lives in society, on the job and off it. His own life, inevitably, is part of his subject matter. Men being what they are, sociologists too manage to segregate their professional insights from their everyday affairs. But it is a rather difficult feat to perform in good faith.

The sociologist moves in the common world of men, close to what most of them would call real. The categories he employs in his analyses are only refinements of the categories by which other men live—power, class, status, race, ethnicity. As a result, there is a deceptive simplicity and obviousness about some sociological investigations. One reads them, nods at the familiar scene, remarks that one has heard all this before and don't people have better things to do than to waste their time on truisms—until one is suddenly brought up against an insight that radically questions everything one had previously assumed about this familiar scene. This is the point at which one begins to sense the excitement of sociology.

Let us take a specific example. Imagine a sociology class in a Southern college where almost all the students are white Southerners. Imagine a lecture on the subject of the racial system of the South. The lecturer is talking here of matters that have been familiar to his students from the time of their infancy. Indeed, it may be that they are much more familiar with the minutiae of this system than he is. They are quite bored as a result. It seems to them that he is only using more pretentious words to describe what they already know. Thus he may use the term "caste," one commonly used now by

American sociologists to describe the Southern racial system. But in explaining the term he shifts to traditional Hindu society, to make it clearer. He then goes on to analyze the magical beliefs inherent in caste tabus, the social dynamics of commensalism and connubium, the economic interests concealed within the system, the way in which religious beliefs relate to the tabus, the effects of the caste system upon the industrial development of the society and vice versa—all in India. But suddenly India is not very far away at all. The lecture then goes back to its Southern theme. The familiar now seems not quite so familiar any more. Questions are raised that are new, perhaps raised angrily, but raised all the same. And at least some of the students have begun to understand that there are functions involved in this business of race that they have not read about in the newspapers (at least not those in their hometowns) and that their parents have not told them—partly, at least, because neither the newspapers nor the parents knew about them.

It can be said that the first wisdom of sociology is this—things are not what they seem. This too is a deceptively simple statement. It ceases to be simple after a while. Social reality turns out to have many layers of meaning. The discovery of each new layer changes the perception of the whole.

Anthropologists use the term "culture shock" to describe the impact of a totally new culture upon a newcomer. In an extreme instance such shock will be experienced by the Western explorer who is told, halfway through dinner, that he is eating the nice old lady he had been chatting with the previous day—a shock with predictable physiological if not moral consequences. Most explorers no longer encounter cannibalism in their travels today. However, the first encounters with polygamy or with puberty rites or even with the way some nations drive their automobiles can be quite a shock to an American visitor. With the shock may go not only disapproval or disgust but a sense of excitement that things can *really* be that different from what they are at home. To some extent, at least, this is the excitement of any first travel abroad. The experience of sociological discovery could be described as "culture shock" minus geographical displacement. In other words, the sociologist travels at home—with shocking results. He is unlikely to find that he is eating a nice old lady for dinner. But the discovery, for instance, that his own church has considerable money invested in the missile industry or that a few blocks from his home there are people who engage in cultic orgies may not be drastically different in emotional impact. Yet we would not want to imply that sociological discoveries are always or even usually outrageous to moral sentiment. Not at all. What they have in common with exploration in distant lands, however, is the sudden illumination of new and unsuspected facets of human existence in society. This is the excitement and, as we shall try to show later, the humanistic justification of sociology.

People who like to avoid shocking discoveries, who prefer to believe that society is just what they were taught in Sunday School, who like the safety of the rules and the maxims of what Alfred Schuetz has called the "world-taken-for-granted," should stay away from sociology. People who feel no temptation before closed doors, who have no curiosity about human beings, who are content to admire scenery without wondering about the people who live in those houses on the other side of that river, should probably also stay away from sociology. They will find it unpleasant or, at any rate, unrewarding. People who are interested in human beings only if they can change, convert or reform them should also be warned, for they will find sociology much less useful than they hoped. And people whose interest is mainly in their own conceptual constructions will do just as well to turn to the study of little white mice. Sociology will do just as well to turn to the study of little mice. Sociology will be satisfying, in the long run, only to those who can think of nothing more entrancing than to watch men and to understand things human.

*   *   *

To be sure, sociology is an individual pastime in the sense that it interests some men and bores others. Some like to observe human beings, others to experiment with mice. The world is big enough to hold all kinds and there is no logical priority for one interest as against another. But the word "pastime" is weak in describing what we mean. Sociology is more like a passion. The sociological perspective is more like a demon that possesses one, that drives one compellingly, again and again, to the questions that are its own. An introduction to sociology is, therefore, an invitation to a very special kind of passion.

STUDY QUESTIONS

1. According to Berger, what is a sociologist?

2. Why does Berger state that **sociology** is a passion?

3. If you had the chance to become a sociologist, what topics would you like to do research on? Please discuss.

4. Please visit the American Sociological Association website to learn more about sociology and what sociologists do (www.asanet.org). Are there areas of sociology to which you think you could contribute? Which areas and specializations seem foreign to you?

MARVIN HARRIS

India's Sacred Cow

n certain instances, for example when we travel abroad, we tend to use our own cultural background to make sense of the cultural practices of the place we are visiting. Some of the cultural practices seem strange, sometimes irrational. It takes a **sociological imagination** to dig deeper and understand that **culture** is how we adapt to the **environment** and the world around us. Marvin Harris traces the history of one cultural practice that may seem strange to Westerners to its logical end in this interesting selection.

NEWS PHOTOGRAPHERS THAT CAME OUT OF INDIA DURING THE famine of the late 1960s showed starving people stretching out bony hands to beg for food while sacred cattle strolled behind undisturbed. The Hindu, it seems, would rather starve to death than eat his cow or even deprive it of food. The cattle appear to browse unhindered through urban markets eating an orange here, a mango there, competing with people for meager supplies of food.

By Western standards, spiritual values seem more important to Indians than life itself. Specialists in food habits around the world like Fred Simons at the University of California at Davis consider Hinduism an irrational ideology that compels people to overlook abundant, nutritious foods for scarcer, less healthful foods.

What seems to be an absurd devotion to the mother cow pervades Indian life. Indian wall calendars portray beautiful young women with bodies of fat white cows, often with milk jetting from their teats into sacred shrines.

Cow worship even carries over into politics. In 1966 a crowd of 120,000 people, led by holy men, demonstrated in front of the Indian House of Parliament in support of the All-Party Cow Protection Campaign Committee. In Nepal, the only contemporary Hindu kingdom, cow slaughter is severely punished. As one story goes, the car driven by an official of a United States agency struck and killed a cow. In order to avoid the international incident that would have occurred when the official was arrested for murder, the Nepalese magistrate concluded that the cow had committed suicide.

Many Indians agree with Western assessments of the Hindu reverence for their cattle, the zebu, or *Bos indicus*, a large-humped species prevalent in Asia and Africa. M. N. Srinivas, an Indian anthropologist, states: "Orthodox Hindu opinion regards the killing of cattle with abhorrence, even though the refusal to kill vast numbers of useless cattle which exist in India today is detrimental to the nation." Even the Indian Ministry of Information formerly maintained that "the large animal population is more a liability than an asset in view of our land resources." Accounts from many different sources point to the same conclusion: India, one of the world's great civilizations, is being strangled by its love for the cow.

The easy explanation for India's devotion to the cow, the one most Westerners and Indians would offer, is that cow worship is an integral part of Hinduism. Religion is somehow good for the soul, even it if sometimes fails the body. Religion orders the cosmos and explains our place in the universe. Religious beliefs, many would claim, have existed for thousands of years and have a life of their own. They are not understandable in scientific terms.

But all this ignores history. There is more to be said for cow worship than is immediately apparent. The earliest Vedas, the Hindu sacred texts from the second millennium B.C., do not prohibit the slaughter of cattle. Instead, they ordain it as part of sacrificial rites. The early Hindus did not avoid the flesh of cows and bulls; they ate it at ceremonial feasts presided over by Brahman priests. Cow worship is a relatively recent development in India; it evolved as the Hindu religion developed and changed.

This evolution is recorded in royal edicts and religious texts written during the last 3,000 years of Indian history. The Vedas from the first millennium B.C. contain contradictory passages, some referring to ritual slaughter and others to a strict taboo on beef consumption. A. N. Bose, in *Social and Rural Economy of Northern India*, 600 B.C.–200 A.D., concludes that many of the sacred-cow passages were incorporated into the texts by priests of a later period.

By 200 A.D. the status of Indian cattle had undergone a spiritual transformation. The Brahman priesthood exhorted the population to venerate the cow and forbade them to abuse it or to feed on it. Religious feasts involving the ritual slaughter and consumption of livestock were eliminated and meat eating was restricted to the nobility.

By 1000 A.D., all Hindus were forbidden to eat beef. Ahimsa, the Hindu belief in the unity of all life, was the spiritual justification for this restriction. But it is difficult to ascertain exactly when this change occurred. An important event that helped to shape the modern complex was the Islamic invasion, which took place in the eighth century A.D. Hindus may have found it politically expedient to set themselves off from the invaders, who were beefeaters, by emphasizing the need to prevent the slaughter of their sacred animals. Thereafter, the cow taboo assumed its modern form and began to function much as it does today.

The place of the cow in modern India is every place—on posters, in the movies, in brass figures, in stone and wood carvings, on the streets, in the fields. The cow is a symbol of health and abundance. It provides the milk that Indians consume in the form of yogurt and ghee (clarified butter), which contribute subtle flavors to much spicy Indian food.

This, perhaps, is the practical role of the cow, but cows provide less than half the milk produced in India. Most cows in India are not dairy breeds. In most regions, when an Indian farmer wants a steady, high-quality source of milk he usually invests in a female water buffalo. In India the water buffalo is the specialized dairy breed because its milk has a higher butterfat content than zebu milk. Although the farmer milks his zebu cows, the milk is merely a by-product.

More vital than zebu milk to South Asian farmers are zebu calves. Male calves are especially valued because from bulls come oxen, which are the mainstay of the Indian agricultural system.

Small, fast oxen drag wooden plows through late-spring fields when monsoons have dampened the dry, cracked earth. After harvest, the oxen break the grain from the stalk by stomping through mounds of cut wheat and rice. For rice cultivation in irrigated fields, the male water buffalo is preferred (it pulls better in deep mud), but for most other crops, including rainfall rice, wheat, sorghum, and millet, and for transporting goods and people to and from town, a team of oxen is preferred. The ox is the Indian peasant's tractor, thresher and family car combined; the cow is the factory that produces the ox.

If draft animals instead of cows are counted, India appears to have too few domesticated ruminants, not too many. Since each of the 70 million farms in India require a draft team, it follows that Indian peasants should use 140 million animals in the fields. But there are only 83 million oxen and male water buffalo on the subcontinent, a shortage of 30 million draft teams.

In other regions of the world, joint ownership of draft animals might overcome a shortage, but Indian agriculture is closely tied to the monsoon rains of late spring and summer. Field preparation and planting must coincide with the rain, and a farmer must have his animals ready to plow when the weather is right. When the farmer without a draft team needs bullocks most, his neighbors are all using theirs. Any delay in turning the soil drastically lowers production.

Because of this dependence on draft animals, loss of the family oxen is devastating. If a beast dies, the farmer must borrow money to buy or rent an ox at interest rates so high that he ultimately loses his land. Every year foreclosures force thousands of poverty-stricken peasants to abandon the countryside for the overcrowded cities.

If a family is fortunate enough to own a fertile cow, it will be able to rear replacements for a lost team and thus survive until life returns to normal. If, as sometimes happens, famine leads a family to sell its cow and ox team, all ties to agriculture are cut. Even if the family survives, it has no way to farm the land, no oxen to work the land, and no cows to produce oxen.

The prohibition against eating meat applies to the flesh of cows, bulls, and oxen, but the cow is the most sacred because it can produce the other two. The peasant whose cow dies is not only crying over a spiritual loss but over the loss of his farm as well.

Religious laws that forbid the slaughter of cattle promote the recovery of the agricultural system from the dry Indian winter and from periods of drought. The monsoon, on which all agriculture depends, is erratic. Sometimes, it arrives early, sometimes late, sometimes not at all. Drought has struck large portions of India time and again in this century, and Indian farmers and the zebus are accustomed to these natural disasters. Zebus can pass weeks on end with little or no food and water. Like camels, they store both in their humps and recuperate quickly with only a little nourishment.

During drought the cows often stop lactating and become barren. In some cases the condition is permanent but often it is only temporary. If barren animals were summarily eliminated, as Western experts in animal husbandry have suggested, cows capable of recovery would be lost along with those entirely debilitated. By keeping alive the cows that can later produce oxen, religious laws against cow slaughter assure the recovery of the agricultural system from the greatest challenge it faces—the failure of the monsoon.

The local Indian governments aid the process of recovery by maintaining homes for barren cows. Farmers reclaim any animal that calves or begins to lactate. One police station in Madras collects strays and pastures them in a field adjacent to the station. After a small fine is paid, a cow is returned to its rightful owner when the owner thinks the cow shows signs of being able to reproduce.

During the hot, dry spring months most of India is like a desert. Indian farmers often complain they cannot feed their livestock during this period. They maintain the cattle by letting them scavenge on the sparse grass along the roads. In the cities the cattle are encouraged to scavenge near food stalls to supplement their scant diet. These are the wandering cattle tourists report seeing throughout India.

Westerners expect shopkeepers to respond to these intrusions with the deference due a sacred animal; instead, their response is a string of curses and the crack of a long bamboo pole across the beast's back or a poke at its genitals. Mahatma Gandhi was well aware of the treatment sacred cows (and bulls and oxen) received in India. "How we bleed her to take the last drop of milk from her. How we starve her to emaciation, how we ill-treat the calves, how we deprive them of their portion of milk, how cruelly we treat the oxen, how we castrate them, how we beat them, how we overload them" [Gandhi, 1954].

Oxen generally receive better treatment than cows. When food is in short supply, thrifty Indian peasants feed their working bullocks and ignore their cows, but rarely do they abandon the cows to die. When cows are sick, farmers worry over them as they would over members of the family and nurse them as if they were children. When the rains return and when the fields are harvested, the farmers again feed their cows regularly and reclaim their abandoned animals. The prohibition against beef consumption is a form of disaster insurance for all India.

Western agronomists and economists are quick to protest that all the functions of the zebu cattle can be improved with organized breeding programs, cultivated pastures, and silage. Because stronger oxen would pull the plow faster, they could work multiple plots of land, allowing farmers to share their animals. Fewer healthy, well-fed cows could provide Indians with more milk. But pastures and silage require arable land, land needed to produce wheat and rice.

A look at Western cattle farming makes plain the cost of adopting advanced technology in Indian agriculture. In a study of livestock production in the United States, David Pimentel of the College of Agriculture and Life Sciences at Cornell University, found that 91 percent of the cereal, legume, and vegetable protein suitable for human consumption is consumed by livestock. Approximately three quarters of the arable land in the United States is devoted to growing food for livestock. In the production of meat and milk, American ranchers use enough fossil fuel to equal more than 82 million barrels of oil annually.

Indian cattle do not drain the system in the same way. In a 1971 study of livestock in West Bengal, Stewart Odend'hal [1972] of the University of Missouri found that Bengalese cattle ate only the inedible remains of subsistence crops—rice straw, rice hulls, the tops of sugar cane, and mustard-oil cake. Cattle graze in the fields after harvest and eat the remains of crops left on the ground; they forage for grass and weeds on the roadsides. The food for zebu cattle costs the human population virtually nothing. "Basically," Odend'hal says, "the cattle convert the items of little direct human value into products of immediate utility."

In addition to plowing the fields and producing milk, the zebus produce dung, which fires the hearths and fertilizes the fields of India. Much of the estimated 800 million tons of manure produced annually is collected by the farmers' children as they follow the family cows and bullocks from place to place. And when the children see the droppings of another farmer's cattle along the road, they pick those up also. Odend'hal reports that the system operates with such high efficiency that the children of West Bengal recover nearly 100 percent of the dung produced by their livestock.

From 40 to 70 percent of all manure produced by Indian cattle is used as fuel for cooking; the rest is returned to the fields as fertilizer. Dried dung burns slowly, cleanly, and with low heat—characteristics that satisfy the household needs of Indian women.

Staples like curry and rice can simmer for hours. While the meal slowly cooks over an unattended fire, the women of the household can do other chores. Cow chips, unlike firewood, do not scorch as they burn.

It is estimated that the dung used for cooking fuel provides the energy-equivalent of 43 million tons of coal. At current prices, it would cost India an extra 1.5 billion dollars in foreign exchange to replace the dung with coal. And if the 350 million tons of manure that are being used as fertilizer were replaced with commercial fertilizers, the expense would be even greater. Roger Revelle of the University of California at San Diego has calculated that 89 percent of the energy used in Indian agriculture (the equivalent of about 140 million tons of coal) is provided by local sources. Even if foreign loans were to provide the money, the capital outlay necessary to replace the Indian cow with tractors and fertilizers for the fields, coal for the fires, and transportation for the family would probably warp international financial institutions for years.

Instead of asking the Indians to learn from the American model of industrial agriculture, American farmers might learn energy conservation from the Indians. Every step in an energy cycle results in a loss of energy to the system. Like a pendulum that slows a bit with each swing, each transfer of energy from sun to plants, plants to animals, and animals to human beings involves energy losses. Some systems are more efficient than others; they provide a higher percentage of the energy inputs in a final, useful form. Seventeen percent of all energy zebus consume is returned in the form of milk, traction, and dung. American cattle raised on Western rangeland return only 4 percent of the energy they consume.

But the American system is improving. Based on techniques pioneered by Indian scientists, at least one commercial firm in the United States is reported to be building plants that will turn manure from cattle feedlots into combustible gas. When organic matter is broken down by anaerobic bacteria, methane gas and carbon dioxide are produced. After the methane is cleansed of the carbon dioxide, it is available for the same purposes as natural gas—cooking, heating, electric generation. The company constructing the biogasification plant plans to sell its product to a gas-supply company, to be piped through the existing distribution system. Schemes similar to this one could make cattle ranches almost independent of utility and gasoline companies; for methane can be used to run trucks, tractors, and cars as well as to supply heat and electricity. The relative energy self-sufficiency that the Indian peasant has achieved is a goal American farmers and industry are now striving for.

Studies like Odend'hal's understate the efficiency of the Indian cow, because dead cows are used for purposes that Hindus prefer not to acknowledge. When a cow dies, an Untouchable, a member of one of the lowest ranking castes in India, is summoned to haul away the carcass. Higher castes consider the body of the dead cow polluting; if they handle it, they must go through a rite of purification.

Untouchables first skin the dead animal and either tan the skin themselves or sell it to a leather factory. In the privacy of their homes, contrary to the teachings of Hinduism, untouchable castes cook the meat and eat it. Indians of all castes rarely acknowledge the existence of these practices to non-Hindus, but most are aware that beefeating takes place. The prohibition against beefeating restricts consumption by the higher castes and helps distribute animal protein to the poorest sectors of the population that otherwise would have no source of these vital nutrients.

Untouchables are not the only Indians who consume beef. Indian Muslims and Christians are under no restriction that forbids them beef, and its consumption is legal in many places. The Indian ban on cow slaughter is state, not national, law and not all states restrict it. In many cities, such as New Delhi, Calcutta, and Bombay, legal slaughterhouses sell beef to retail customers and to restaurants that serve steak.

If the caloric value of beef and the energy costs involved in the manufacture of synthetic leather were included in the estimate of energy, the calculated efficiency of Indian livestock would rise considerably. As well as the system works, experts often claim that its efficiency can be further improved. Alan Heston [et al., 1971], an economist at the University of Pennsylvania, believes that Indians suffer from an overabundance of cows simply because they refuse to slaughter the excess cattle. India could produce at least the same number of oxen and the same quantities of milk and manure with 30 million fewer cows. Heston calculates that only 40 cows are necessary to maintain a population of 100 bulls and oxen. Since India averages 70 cows for every 100 bullocks, the difference, 30 million cows, is expendable.

What Heston fails to note is that sex ratios among cattle in different regions of India vary tremendously, indicating that adjustments in the cow population do take place. Along the Ganges River, one of the holiest shrines of Hinduism, the ratio drops to 47 cows for every 100 male animals. This ratio reflects the preference for dairy buffalo in the irrigated sectors of the Gangetic Plains. In nearby Pakistan, in contrast, where cow slaughter is permitted, the sex ratio is 60 cows to 100 oxen.

Since the sex ratios among cattle differ greatly from region to region and do not even approximate the balance that would be expected if no females were killed, we can assume that some culling of herds does take place; Indians do adjust their religious restrictions to accommodate ecological realities.

They cannot kill a cow but they can tether an old or unhealthy animal until it has starved to death. They cannot slaughter a calf but they can yoke it with a large wooden triangle so that when it nurses it irritates the mother's udder and gets kicked to death. They cannot ship their animals to the slaughterhouse but they can sell them to Muslims, closing their eyes to the fact that the Muslims will take the cattle to the slaughterhouse.

These violations of the prohibition against cattle slaughter strengthen the premise that cow worship is a vital part of Indian culture. The practice arose to prevent the population from consuming the animal on which Indian agriculture depends. During the first millennium B.C., the Gange Valley became one of the most densely populated regions of the world.

Where previously there had been only scattered villages, many towns and cities arose and peasants farmed every available acre of land. Kingsley Davis, a population expert at the University of California at Berkeley, estimates that by 300 B.C. between 50 million and 100 million people were living in India. The forested Ganges Valley became a windswept semidesert and signs of ecological collapse appeared; droughts and floods became commonplace, erosion took away the rich topsoil, farms shrank as population increased, and domesticated animals became harder and harder to maintain.

It is probable that the elimination of meat eating came about in a slow, practical manner. The farmers who decided not to eat their cows, who saved them for procreation to produce oxen, were the ones who survived the natural disasters. Those who ate beef lost the tools with which to farm. Over a period of centuries, more and more farmers probably avoided beef until an unwritten taboo came into existence.

Only later was the practice codified by the priesthood. While Indian peasants were probably aware of the role of cattle in their society, strong sanctions were necessary to protect zebus from a population faced with starvation. To remove temptation, the flesh of cattle became taboo and the cow became sacred.

The sacredness of the cow is not just an ignorant belief that stands in the way of progress. Like all concepts of the sacred and the profane, this one affects the physical world; it defines the relationships that are important for the maintenance of Indian society.

Indians have the sacred cow, we have the "sacred" car and the "sacred" dog. It would not occur to us to propose the elimination of automobiles and dogs from our society without carefully considering the consequences, and we should not propose the elimination of zebu cattle without first understanding their place in the social order of India.

Human society is neither random nor capricious. The regularities of thought and behavior called culture are the principal mechanisms by which we human beings adapt to the world around us. Practices and beliefs can be rational or irrational, but a society that fails to adapt to its environment is doomed to extinction. Only those societies that draw the necessities of life from their surroundings without destroying those surroundings inherit the earth. The West has much to learn from the great antiquity of Indian civilization, and the sacred cow is an important part of that lesson.

REFERENCES

Gandhi, Mohandas K. 1954. *How to Serve the Cow*. Bombay: Navajivan Publishing House.

Heston, Alan, et al. 1971. "An Approach to the Sacred Cow of India," *Current Anthropology* 12, 191–209.

Odend'hal, Stewart. 1972. "Gross Energetic Efficiency of Indian Cattle in Their Environment." *Journal of Human Ecology* 1, 1–27.

STUDY QUESTIONS

1. What is the easy explanation for India's devotion to the cow? What is a more complex view?

2. Why does the author state that "human **society** is neither random nor capricious"?

3. Think about a peculiar practice from your **culture** (e.g., cosmetic plastic surgery); using Harris's narrative, write about the ways the society you live in makes a behavior rational.

4. As a group, discuss what things in your culture are comparable to the Indian sacred cow.

GEORGE RITZER

The "McDonaldization" of Society

alk into any McDonald's with money in one hand and a number written on the other one and they'll feed you without your saying a word. The food you'll get will taste exactly like it does anywhere else in the country. Stay at a chain hotel anywhere in the country, and you'll find the same beds, the same carpets, and the same powdered eggs for breakfast. Drive to the suburbs, and you'll see house after house with the same facade, same floor plan, and same mailbox. This predictability is just one quality of what George Ritzer has called the "McDonaldized Society." In this landmark piece Ritzer discusses this trend toward the increased **rationalization** of the world and the consequences of this process.

A WIDE-RANGING PROCESS OF *RATIONALIZATION* IS OCCURRING across American society and is having an increasingly powerful impact in many other parts of the world. It encompasses such disparate phenomena as fast food restaurants, TV dinners, packaged tours, industrial robots, plea bargaining and open-heart surgery on an assembly-line basis. As widespread and as important as these developments are, it is clear that we have barely begun a process that promises even more extraordinary changes (e.g., genetic engineering) in the years to come. We can think of rationalization as a historical process and rationality as the end result of that development. As an historical process, rationalization has distinctive roots in the western world. Writing in the late 19th and early 20th centuries, the great German sociologist Max Weber saw his society as the center of the ongoing process of rationalization

"The 'McDonaldization of Society'" by George Ritzer from *Journal of American Culture*, Vol. 27, No. 3 (September 2004), pages 100–107. Copyright © 2004 Wiley Periodicals Inc. Reproduced with permission from Blackwell Publishing Ltd.

and the bureaucracy as its paradigm case. The model of rationalization, at least in contemporary America, is no longer the bureaucracy, but might be better thought of as the fast food restaurant. As a result, our concern here is with what might be termed the "McDonaldization of Society." While the fast food restaurant is not the ultimate expression of rationality, it is the current exemplar for future developments in rationalization.

A society characterized by rationality is one which emphasizes *efficiency, predictability, calculability, substitution of non-human for human technology* and *control over uncertainty*. In discussing the various dimensions of rationalization, we will be little concerned with the gains already made, and yet to be realized, by greater rationalization. These advantages are widely discussed in schools and in the mass media. In fact, we are in danger of being seduced by the innumerable advantages already offered, and promised in the future, by rationalization. The glitter of these accomplishments and promises has served to distract most people from the grave dangers posed by progressive rationalization. In other words, we are ultimately concerned here with the irrational consequences that often flow from rational systems. Thus, the second major theme of this essay might be termed "the irrationality of rationality."

In spite of the emphasis here on the problems posed by rationalization, this will not be one of those pleas for a return to a less rationalized way of life. Although there is certainly room for less rationalized pockets in a rational society, in most cases we cannot, and should not, try to reverse the process of rationalization. In our rush to critique rationalization we cannot ignore its many advantages (McDonald's does offer a lot of tasty food at relatively low cost). Furthermore, we should not romanticize the "noble" life of the pre-rational society with its many problems and disadvantages. We would not, in most cases, want to recreate a life beset by these problems, even if it was possible to do so. Instead, what we need do is gain a better understanding of the process of rationalization so that we can come to exercise more and better control over it.

Although we will discuss rationalization as a distinct process, we do not want to convey the impression that it is some mystical process that is, under its own momentum, sweeping through the world altering everything and everyone in its path. There are individuals, groups and organizations that are acting in various ways to foster the development and expansion of rationalization. For a wide range of reasons, they have found it in their interest to foster rationalization. Although profit is often a powerful motive for rationalization, it does not adequately explain many rational developments in capitalist societies (e.g., in schools, religious groups) and it certainly does not explain the widespread expansion of rational systems in socialist and communist societies.

The objective through most of the rest of this essay is to examine the nature of each of the major dimensions of rationalization and to illustrate the ubiquity of the process by offering a wide range of examples for each. Not only shall we discuss each of the dimensions of rationalization—efficiency, predictability, calculability, substitution of non-human for human technology and greater control over uncertainty—we will also discuss a seemingly inevitable byproduct of rationality—the irrationality of rationality.

EFFICIENCY

The process of rationalization leads to a society in which a great deal of emphasis is placed on finding the best or optimum means to any given end. Whatever a group of people define as an end, and everything they so define, is to be pursued by attempting to find the best means to achieve the end. Thus, in the Germany of Weber's day, the bureaucracy was seen as the most efficient means of handling a wide array of administrative tasks. Somewhat later, the Nazis came to develop the concentration camp, its ovens and other devices as the optimum method of collecting and murdering millions of Jews and other people. The efficiency that Weber described in turn-of-the-century Germany, and which later came to characterize many Nazi activities, has become a basic principle of life in virtually every sector of a rational society.

The modern American family, often with two wage earners, has little time to prepare elaborate meals. For the relatively few who still cook such meals, there is likely to be great reliance on cookbooks that make cooking from scratch much more efficient. However, such cooking is relatively rare today. Most families take as their objective quickly and easily prepared meals. To this end, much use is made of pre-packaged meals and frozen TV dinners.

For many modern families, the TV dinner is no longer efficient enough. To many people, eating out, particularly in a fast food restaurant, is a far more efficient way of obtaining their meals. Fast food restaurants capitalize on this by being organized so that diners are fed as efficiently as possible. They offer a limited, simple menu that can be cooked and served in an assembly-line fashion. The latest development in fast food restaurants, the addition of drive-through windows, constitutes an effort to increase still further the efficiency of the dining experience. The family now can simply drive through, pick up its order, and eat it while driving to the next, undoubtedly efficiently organized, activity. The success of the fast food restaurant has come full circle with frozen food manufacturers now touting products for the home modeled after those served in fast food restaurants.

Increasingly, efficiently organized food production and distribution systems lie at the base of the ability of people to eat their food efficiently at home, in the fast food restaurant, or in their cars. Farms, groves, ranches, slaughter houses, warehouses, transportation systems, and retailers are all oriented toward increasing efficiency. A notable example is chicken production where they are mass bred, force fed (often with many chemicals), slaughtered on an assembly line, iced or fast frozen and shipped to all parts of the country. Some may argue that such chickens do not taste as good as the fresh-killed, local variety, but their complaints are likely to be drowned in a flood of mass-produced chickens. Then there is bacon which is more efficiently shipped, stored and sold when it is preserved by sodium nitrate, a chemical which is unfortunately thought by many to be carcinogenic. Whatever one may say about the quality or the danger of the products, the fact remains that they are all shaped by the drive for efficiency.

Once the goods have reached the marketplace they need to be purchased. Over the centuries we have witnessed an increase in the efficiency of the means of exchange. We have come a long way from the inefficient method whereby people had to bring their goats to market in order to exchange them for clothing. Since then we have gone from precious metals to coins to bills and to checking accounts, to the development of credit cards and the replacement of bills and checks by the more efficiently used plastic money and computer.

The fast food restaurant is certainly not the only place one can spend money. The center of spending is now the modern shopping center and the supermarket. These are organized in a highly efficient manner in order to aid business. Supermarkets have grown even more efficient recently with the advent of computer scanning devices which expedite the checkout process and, at the same time, make the work of stockpeople more efficient by eliminating the need to stamp prices on the items.

When our shoppers return home (in efficiently produced cars and on efficiently built roads) they are likely to enter apartments or suburban tract houses which have been efficiently constructed. Among other things, this means there is little or nothing to distinguish one apartment or house from many others. In constructing such dwellings, esthetic elements like trees or hills are likely to be leveled if they stand in the way of efficient construction.

In the morning, the parents are likely to troop off to work in a variety of occupational settings in which an effort has been made to maximize the efficiency of operation. The roots of these efforts lie in Henry Ford's assembly-line and F.W. Taylor's principles of scientific management. Both were developed at the turn of the century to be applied largely to manual work. Although blue collar work remains the focus of these efforts, many white collar and professional occupations have been made more efficient in accord with ideas that trace their roots to Ford and Taylor.

While the parents are off to work, the children are headed to schools in which the specialization of classes, the platoon system, and mass classes are all designed to increase the efficiency in which students are processed through the educational system. The small class, to say nothing of the one-to-one tutorial, are disappearing since they are inefficient.

If the family is unhappy with the efficiency that pervades virtually every facet of daily life, it might seek relief in leisure-time activities that it may assume to be immune from the process of rationalization. However, even in these areas, the principles of efficiency are omnipresent. International travel is affordable for many only through organized tours that efficiently transport large groups of tourists from one site to another. The modern amusement park is often little more than a vast, elaborate people-moving machine designed to transport people through the park and its various attractions as efficiently as possible. Campgrounds, trout farms, sporting events and night clubs are other examples of entertainment that have grown increasingly efficient.

One of the most interesting and important aspects of efficiency is that it often comes to be not a means but an end in itself. This "displacement of goals" is a major problem in a rationalizing society. We have, for example, the bureaucrats who slavishly follow the rules even though their inflexibility negatively affects the organization's ability to achieve its goals. Then there are the bureaucrats who are so concerned with efficiency that they lose sight of the ultimate goals the means are designed to achieve. A good example was the Nazi concentration camp officers who, in devoting so much attention to maximizing the efficiency of the camps' operation, lost sight of the fact that the ultimate purpose of the camps was the murder of millions of people.

PREDICTABILITY

A second component of rationalization involves the effort to ensure predictability from one place to another. In a rational society, people want to know what to expect when they enter a given setting or acquire some sort of commodity. They neither want nor expect surprises. They want to know that if they journey to another locale, the setting they enter or the commodity they buy will be essentially the same as the setting they entered or product they purchased earlier. Furthermore, people want to be sure that what they encounter is much like what they encountered at earlier times. In order to ensure predictability over time and place a rational society must emphasize such things as discipline, order, systemization, formalization, routine, consistency and methodical operation.

One of the attractions of TV dinners for modern families is that they are highly predictable. The TV dinner composed of fried chicken, mashed potatoes, green peas and peach cobbler is exactly the same from one time to another and one city to another. Home cooking from scratch is, conversely, a notoriously unpredictable enterprise with little assurance that dishes will taste the same time after time. However, the cookbook cannot eliminate all unpredictability. There are often simply too many ingredients and other variables involved. Thus the cookbook dish is far less predictable than the TV dinner or a wide array of other prepared dishes.

Fast food restaurants rank very high on the dimension of predictability. In order to help ensure consistency, the fast food restaurant offers only a limited menu. Predictable end-products are made possible by the use of similar raw materials, technologies and preparation and serving techniques. Not only the food is predictable; the physical structures, the logo, the "ambience" and even the personnel are as well.

The food that is shipped to our homes and our fast food restaurants is itself affected by the process of increasing predictability. Thus our favorite white bread is indistinguishable from one place to another. In fact, food producers have made great efforts to ensure such predictability.

On packaged tours travelers can be fairly sure that the people they travel with will be much like themselves. The planes, busses, hotel accommodations, restaurants, and at least the way in which the sites are visited are very similar from one location to another. Many people go on packaged tours *because* they are far more predictable than travel undertaken on an individual basis.

Amusement parks used to be highly unpredictable affairs. People could never be sure, from one park to another, precisely what sorts of rides, events, foods, visitors, and employees they would encounter. All of that has changed in the era of the theme parks inspired by Disneyland. Such parks seek to ensure predictability in various ways. For example, a specific type of young person is hired in these parks, and they are all trained in much the same way, so that they have a robot-like predictability.

Other leisure-time activities have grown similarly predictable. Camping in the wild is loaded with uncertainties—bugs, bears, rain, cold and the like. To make camping more predictable, organized grounds have sprung up around the country. Gone are many of the elements of unpredictability replaced by RV's, paved over parking lots, sanitized campsites, fences and enclosed camp centers that provide laundry and food services, recreational activities, television and video games. Sporting events, too, have in a variety of ways been made more predictable. The use of artificial turf in baseball makes for a more predictable bounce of a ball.

Many of the jobs, occupations and careers in which people work are among the most predictable elements of American society. This predictability is traceable to many sources, but two of the most important are scientific management and the assembly line. The principles of scientific management emphasize, among other things, that there is one, and only one, best way to do a job. The idea is for the efficiency expert to discover that one best way, then institutionalize it. Of course, the predictability that stems from the assembly line, like every other segment of the rationalization process, is not without its problems and irrationalities, especially in this case the negative effect such a system has on workers: the classic alienation of the assembly-line worker.

The technology of the assembly line, and the predictability it produces, is now being extended to many, often unlikely, domains. Even open-heart surgery by the most famous heart surgeon, Dr. Denton Cooley, is being performed in a kind of assembly-line fashion. Each day a number of patients are prepared in a number of different operating rooms, preliminary steps are taken by highly specialized personnel, Cooley arrives to perform the most delicate steps and then he moves on to the next room to perform the same steps while assistants complete the process on the preceding patient. Open-heart surgery has been turned into a highly predictable process and one that is fraught with much less uncertainty for both patient and surgeon.

CALCULABILITY OR QUANTITY RATHER THAN QUALITY

It could easily be argued that the emphasis on quantifiable measures, on things that can be counted, is *the* most defining characteristic of a rational society. Quality is notoriously difficult to evaluate. How do we assess the quality of a hamburger, or a physician, or a student? Instead of even trying, in an increasing number of cases, a rational society seeks to develop a series of quantifiable measures that it takes as surrogates for quality. This urge to quantify has given great impetus to the development of the computer and has, in turn, been spurred by the widespread use and increasing sophistication of the computer.

The fact is that many aspects of modern rational society, especially as far as calculable issues are concerned, are made possible and more widespread by the computer. We need not belabor the ability of the computer to handle large numbers of virtually anything, but somewhat less obvious is the use of the computer to give the illusion of personal attention in a world made increasingly impersonal in large part *because* of the computer's capacity to turn virtually everything into quantifiable dimensions. We have all now had many experiences where we open a letter personally addressed to us only to find a computer letter. We are aware that the names and addresses of millions of people have been stored on tape and that with the aid of a number of word processors a form letter has been sent to every name on the list. Although the computer is able to give a sense of personal attention, most people are nothing more than an item on a huge mailing list.

Our main concern here, though, is not with the computer, but with the emphasis on quantity rather than quality that it has helped foster. One of the most obvious examples in the university is the emphasis given to grades and cumulative grade point averages. With less and less contact between professor and student, there is little real effort to assess the quality of what students know, let alone the quality of their overall abilities. Instead, the sole measure of the quality of most college students is their grade in a given course and their grade point averages. Another blatant example is the emphasis on a variety of uniform exams such as SATs and GREs in which the essence of an applicant is reduced to a few simple scores and percentiles.

Within the educational institution, the importance of grades is well known, but somewhat less known is the way quantifiable factors have become an essential part of the process of evaluating college professors. For example, teaching ability is very hard to evaluate. Administrators have difficulty assessing teaching quality and thus substitute quantitative scores. Of course each score involves qualitative judgments, but this is conveniently ignored. Student opinion polls are taken and the scores are summed, averaged and compared. Those who score well are deemed good teachers while those who don't are seen as poor teachers. There are many problems involved in relying on these scores such as the fact that easy teachers in "gut" courses may well obtain high ratings while rigorous teachers of difficult courses are likely to score poorly.

While teaching ratings are important to college professors, a variety of other quantifiable dimensions are of even greater importance. Although the idea of "publish or perish" has never been a completely accurate description of the demands on academics, there is a great deal of emphasis on publications, especially at the major universities. But the quality of academic work is difficult to evaluate, so the emphasis is placed on quantitative measures of academic productivity. One crude measure is the sheer number of articles and books published. Slightly more sophisticated are efforts to weight different kinds of publications (monographs, textbooks, articles in journals of varying prestige) and come up with a total score for each academician that more adequately reflects the differential importance of various kinds of publications. A measure that is gaining increasing support is the number of times an author's works are cited by colleagues. The idea is that the higher the quality of the work, the more likely it is to be cited in colleagues' bibliographies. The fallacy is that, in addition to the general problem of simply trying to reduce quality to a single number, a relatively poor work could get a high citation rating if it is singled out by many for criticism.

In the workworld we find many examples of the effort to substitute quantity for quality. Scientific management was heavily oriented to turning everything work-related into quantifiable dimensions. Instead of relying on the "rule of thumb" of the operator, scientific management sought to develop precise measures of how much work was to be done by each and every motion of the worker. Everything that could be was reduced to numbers and all these numbers were then analyzable using a variety of mathematical formulae. The assembly line is similarly oriented to a variety of quantifiable dimensions such as optimizing the speed of the line, minimizing time for each task, lowering the price of the finished product, increasing sales and ultimately increasing profits. The divisional system pioneered by General Motors and thought to be one of the major reasons for its past success was oriented to the reduction of the performance of each division to a few, bottom-line numbers. By monitoring and comparing these numbers, General Motors was able to exercise control over the results without getting involved in the day-to-day activities of each division.

Quantitative factors are of overwhelming importance in the evaluation and success of television programming. It is the rating system which determines whether television programs will remain on the air. The problem is that there is often an inverse relationship between the quality of a show and its ratings. Shows with little to offer artistically such as *Dallas*, *Love Boat* and the *Dukes of Hazzard*[1] get very high ratings and remain on the air year after year, while high quality shows tend not even to get air time and, if they do, it is often on PBS and with very low ratings.

Sports in general, and baseball in particular, are dominated by an emphasis on numbers. However, in sports there is a closer relationship between quantity and quality than in many other areas of life. The earned run average of a pitcher or the batting average of a batter are fairly good measures of the quality of their play. But even here a number of intangible qualities of play do not show up. For example, a player may be very valuable, even though his statistics are not particularly good, for his ability to make a clutch play, inspire his teammates or be a leader. There are examples in sports where the mania for numbers has adversely affected the quality of the game. In professional basketball a team must shoot the ball within 24 seconds, whereas in most college games a team can take as long to shoot as necessary. This of course leads to more points in pro ball, but many worry that it has turned the game into a mindless "run and gun" activity. The strategy that used to characterize professional basketball, and still is found in college ball, tends to be lost because a team must shoot the ball in such a short period of time.

Politics offers a number of interesting examples of the substitution of quantitative for qualitative measures. Presidential candidates are obsessed by their ratings in the polls and often adjust what they say or do to what the pollsters tell them is likely to increase their ratings. Even sitting presidents (and other politicians) are highly attuned to the polls. The emphasis often seems to be on the impact on the polls of taking a specific political position rather than the qualities of that position.

In foreign policy one area in which we see an absolute mania for numbers is nuclear deterrence. Even though both the United States and the Soviet Union possess arsenals large enough to destroy each other many times over, their efforts to negotiate treaties limiting nuclear weapons often get bogged down in trying to accurately assess the "relative throw weight" of their respective nuclear arms. While accurate measures of throw weight are no doubt important, there is a tendency on both sides to get lost in the minutiae of the numbers and to lose sight of the qualitative fact that both sides have the nuclear might to destroy the other side many times over. There are many other areas, for instance plea bargains in the criminal justice system, in which a quantitative emphasis undoubtedly leads to a number of qualitatively bad decisions.

Thus, the third dimension of rationalization, calculability or the emphasis on quantity rather than quality, has wide applicability to the social world. It is a truly central, if not the central, component of a rationalizing society. To return to our favorite example, it is the case that McDonald's expends far more effort telling us how many billions of hamburgers it has sold than it does in telling us about the quality of those

---

[1] American television series of the late 1970s and early 1980s.

burgers. Relatedly, it touts the size of its product (the "Big Mac") more than the quality of the product (it is not the "Good Mac"). The bottom line in many settings is the number of customers processed, the speed with which they are processed, and the profits produced. Quality is secondary, if indeed there is any concern at all for it.

SUBSTITUTION OF NON-HUMAN TECHNOLOGY

In spite of herculean efforts, there are important limits to the ability to rationalize what human beings think and do. Seemingly no matter what one does, people still retain at least the ultimate capacity to think and act in a variety of unanticipated ways. Thus, in spite of great efforts to make human behavior more efficient, more predictable, more calculable, people continue to act in unforeseen ways. People continue to make home cooked meals from scratch, to camp in tents in the wild, to eat in old-fashioned diners, and to sabotage the assembly-lines. Because of these realities, there is great interest among those who foster increasing rationality in using rational technologies to limit individual independence and ultimately to replace human beings with machines and other technologies that lack the ability to think and act in unpredictable ways.

McDonald's does not yet have robots to serve us food, but it does have teenagers whose ability to act autonomously is almost completely eliminated by techniques, procedures, routines and machines. There are numerous examples of this including rules which prescribe all the things a counterperson should do in dealing with a customer as well as a large variety of technologies which determine the actions of workers such as drink dispensers which shut themselves off when the cup is full; buzzers, lights and bells which indicate when food (e.g., french fries) is done; and cash registers which have the prices of each item programmed in. One of the latest attempts to constrain individual action is Denny's use of pre-measured packages of dehydrated food that are "cooked" simply by putting them under the hot water tap. Because of such tools and machines, as well as the elaborate rules dictating worker behavior, people often feel like they are dealing with human robots when they relate to the personnel of a fast food restaurant. When human robots are found, mechanical robots cannot be far behind. Once people are reduced to a few robot-like actions, it is a relatively easy step to replace them with mechanical robots. Thus Burgerworld is reportedly opening a prototypical restaurant in which mechanical robots serve the food.

Much of the recent history of work, especially manual work, is a history of efforts to replace human technology with non-human technology. Scientific management was oriented to the development of an elaborate and rigid set of rules about how jobs were to be done. The workers were to blindly and obediently follow those rules and not to do the work the way they saw fit. The various skills needed to perform a task were carefully delineated and broken down into a series of routine steps that could be taught to all workers. The skills, in other words, were built into the routines rather than belonging to skilled craftspersons. Similar points can be made about the assembly-line which is basically a set of non-human technologies that have the needed steps and skills built into them. The human worker is reduced to performing a limited number of simple, repetitive operations. However, the control of this technology over the individual worker is so great and omnipresent that individual workers have reacted negatively manifesting such things as tardiness, absenteeism, turnover and even sabotage. We are now witnessing a new stage in this technological development with automated processes now totally replacing many workers with robots. With the coming of robots we have reached the ultimate stage in the replacement of human with non-human technology.

Even religion and religious crusades have not been unaffected by the spread of non-human technologies. The growth of large religious organizations, the use of Madison Avenue techniques, and even drive-in churches all reflect the incursion of modern technology. But it is in the electronic church, religion through the TV screens, that replacement of human by non-human technology in religion is most visible and has its most important manifestation.

Running for president, or any other political office, used to be a highly personal undertaking in which the objective was to see personally, and be seen by, as many voters as possible. Now we have presidential politics waged largely on the TV screens and in accord with routines developed by Madison Avenue public relations types. The technology of the TV spectacular is now being applied to the campaign appearances of presidential candidates. The candidate is most likely to interact with little more than the TV screen and when he does venture out into the real world, it is likely to be only for the images that such a trip will cast on the home screen.

CONTROL

This leads us to the fifth major dimension of rationalization—control. Rational systems are oriented toward, and structured to expedite, control in a variety of senses. At the most general level, we can say that rational systems are set up to allow for greater control over the uncertainties of life—birth, death, food production and distribution, housing, religious salvation and many, many others. More specifically, rational systems are oriented to gaining greater control over the major source of uncertainty in social life—other people. Among other things, this means control over subordinates by superiors and control of clients and customers by workers.

There are many examples of rationalization oriented toward gaining greater control over the uncertainties of life. The burgeoning of the genetic engineering movement can be seen as being aimed at gaining better control over the production of life itself. Similarly, amniocentesis can be seen as a technique which will allow the parents to determine the kind of child they will have. The efforts to rationalize food production and distribution can be seen as being aimed at gaining greater control over the problems of hunger and starvation. A steady and regular supply of food can make life itself more certain for large numbers of people who today live under the threat of death from starvation.

At a more specific level, the rationalization of food preparation and serving at McDonald's gives it great control over its employees. The automobile assembly line has a similar impact. In fact, the vast majority of the structures of a rational society exert extraordinary control over the people who labor in them. But because of the limits that still exist on the degree of control that rational structures can exercise over individuals, many rationalizing employers are driven to seek to more fully rationalize their operations and totally eliminate the worker. The result is an automated, robot-like technology over which, barring some *2001*[2] rebellion, there is almost total control.

In addition to control over employees, rational systems are also interested in controlling the customer/clients they serve. For example, the fast food restaurant with its counter, the absence of waiters and waitresses, the limited seating, and the drive-through windows all tend to lead customers to do certain things and not to do others.

IRRATIONALITY OF RATIONALITY

Although not an inherent part of rationalization, the *irrationality of rationality* is a seemingly inevitable byproduct of the process. We can think of the irrationality of rationality in several ways. At the most general level it can simply be seen as an overarching label for all the negative effects of rationalization. More specifically, it can be seen as the opposite of rationality, at least in some of its senses. For example, there are the inefficiencies and unpredictabilities that are often produced by seemingly rational systems. Thus, although bureaucracies are constructed to bring about greater efficiency in organizational work, the fact is that there are notorious inefficiencies such as the "red tape" associated with the operation of most bureaucracies. Or, take the example of the arms race in which a focus on quantifiable aspects of nuclear weapons may well have made the occurrence of nuclear war more, rather than less, unpredictable.

---

[2] *2001: A Space Odyssey*, 1968 film in which a computer gains extraordinary power.

Of greatest importance, however, is the variety of negative effects that rational systems have on the individuals who live, work and are served by them. We might say that *rational systems are not reasonable systems*. As we've already discussed, rationality brings with it great dehumanization as people are reduced to acting like robots. Among the dehumanizing aspects of a rational society are large lecture classes, computer letters, pray TV, work on the automobile assembly line, and dining at a fast food restaurant. Rationalization also tends to bring with it disenchantment leaving much of our lives without any mystery or excitement. Production by a hand craftsman is far more mysterious than an assembly-line technology where each worker does a single, very limited operation. Camping in an RV tends to suffer in comparison to the joys to be derived from camping in the wild. Overall a fully rational society would be a very bleak and uninteresting place.

In addition to being dehumanizing and disenchanting many rational systems which are supposedly constructed to help people, in the end often have very negative effects. Thus to produce massive amounts of food, producers are driven to rationalize food production in a number of ways including the use of more and more pesticides and artificial ingredients. While such rational technologies are capable of producing a lot of food, they often produce foods that are not as nourishing as their natural counterparts and, in some cases, include chemicals that may be harmful, dangerous and even fatal. McDonald's seemingly rational way of feeding people quickly and cheaply has had many unforeseen and irrational consequences such as weight gain because of the highly caloric nature of the food, increased cholesterol levels, heightened blood pressure as a result of the high salt content of the food, and it has played a key role in the destruction of the family meal and perhaps ultimately the nuclear family.

CONCLUSIONS

Rationalization, with McDonald's as the paradigm case, is occurring throughout America, and, increasingly, other societies. In virtually every sector of society more and more emphasis is placed on efficiency, predictability, calculability, replacement of human by non-human technology, and control over uncertainty. Although progressive rationalization has brought with it innumerable advantages, it has also created a number of problems, the various irrationalities of rationality, which threaten to accelerate in the years to come. These problems, and their acceleration should not be taken as a case for the return to a less rational form of society. Such a return is not only impossible but also undesirable. What is needed is not a less rational society, but greater control over the process of rationalization involving, among other things, efforts to ameliorate its irrational consequences.

STUDY QUESTIONS

1. What does Ritzer mean when he says **society** has become "McDonaldized"?

2. What are the five major components of **rationalization**?

3. What are the irrationalities of the rationality behind the McDonaldization of society?

4. Describe an aspect of your life that has been "McDonaldized" that was not discussed in the text.

MICHAEL L. BENSON

Denying the Guilty Mind:
Accounting for Involvement
in a White-Collar Crime

t's often hard to imagine the motivations of already well-to-do **white-collar criminals**—which is precisely why criminologist Michael L. Benson set out to **interview** such offenders. What Benson found is that the criminals he spoke with denied their criminality, thinking of themselves as businessmen, not convicts. In effect, they employed "neutralization," or detailed excuses, for their behavior, including denying that their **crimes** caused any harm, asserting their alleged crimes were "victimless," or placing the blame on others. Benson reports on thirty convicted, white-collar offenders, showing how this seemingly unique form of criminal behavior fits into existing theories of **deviance**.

THE SUBJECTIVE EXPERIENCES OF THOSE WHO PASS THROUGH the criminal justice system have seldom been given explicit attention by the criminologist.[1] In particular, little attention has been paid to the offender's account of involvement in the offense.[2] In the case of white-collar criminals, the failure to analyze the offender's explanation for involvement in the offense is especially noteworthy. Although white-collar offenders are assumed to suffer subjectively as a result of the public

[1] There is a well-developed literature which treats the subjective experiences of deviants and which has obvious associations with the subject at hand. For examples, see Matza (1969) and Becker (1963). [Unless otherwise noted; notes are those of the author.]

[2] Cressey's (1953) study of embezzlers is an exception to this generalization.

humiliation of adjudication as criminals, they are also assumed, paradoxically, to be able to maintain a noncriminal self-concept and to successfully deny the criminality of their actions (Conklin, 1977).

The present study treats the accounts given by a sample of convicted white-collar offenders, focusing specifically on the techniques they use to deny their own criminality. The emphasis is on general patterns and regularities in the data. The central research question is: How do convicted white-collar offenders account for their adjudication as criminals?[3] While researchers have frequently expressed outrage at the denial of criminality that is thought to be typical of white-collar criminals, few attempts have been made to understand how this process occurs or to relate it to general deviance theory. Rather, researchers have all too often concentrated on morally condemning offenders (Clinard and Yeager, 1978).

Over 30 years ago, Sutherland (1949: 222, 225) wrote,

> Businessmen develop rationalizations which conceal the fact of crime. . . . Even when they violate the law, they do not conceive of themselves as criminals. . . . Businessmen fight whenever words that tend to break down this rationalization are used.

This view of white-collar offenders has continued to the present day (Geis, 1982; Meier and Geis, 1982). Indeed, failure to confront and penetrate the rationalizations used by white-collar offenders and to get beyond a sympathetic view of the individual offender is considered by some to be one of the reasons for the continued widespread prevalence of white-collar crimes (Geis, 1982: 55–57; Meier and Geis, 1982: 98). In addition, others have argued that the leniency with which white-collar criminals are treated by the justice system derives in part from their ability to evoke sympathy from judges (Conklin, 1977).

These widely held beliefs regarding the rationalization processes used by white-collar offenders to justify their crimes and their ability to provoke sympathetic consideration rely, however, on anecdotal evidence. The typical offender studied is a person of extremely high status who has been convicted of a particularly egregious offense. Examples include the studies of former Vice President Agnew (Naughton, Crewdson, Franklin, Lydon, and Solpukas, 1977) and the executives involved in the heavy electrical equipment antitrust case of 1961 (Geis, 1967). These cases are important for symbolic reasons, but the individuals involved most likely do not represent typical white-collar offenders.

High-status offenders tend to receive a great deal of media attention. The cases in which they are involved become public morality plays, and the protagonists become representatives of larger institutional or political constituencies: business versus consumers, governmental regulation versus free enterprise, or employers versus employees. A recent work by Fisse and Braithwaite (1983) gives many examples and is an

---

[3] The term "account" is used here in a special sense developed by Scott and Lyman (1968). It is described in greater detail in a later section of the paper.

important advance in the understanding of how corporate actors attempt to manage the impact of adverse publicity. However, although it is assumed that white-collar offenders are able to maintain a noncriminal self-concept and avoid stigmatization as criminals, the subtle interactional processes whereby individual white-collar offenders attempt to avoid the transformation of their personal and public identities have for the most part been ignored.

Rothman and Gandossy (1982), using quantitative methods, looked at the role the defendant's version of the offense plays in the decision to sanction, finding that the sufficiency of the defendant's story can influence the probation officer's evaluation of the defendant and indirectly the sanction imposed by the judge. The defendant's written version of the offense as it appears in the presentence investigation report was treated as an account.

It is likely that accounts vary depending upon the audience to which they are presented. In preparing his version of the offense, the defendant is talking to the probation officer and to the judge involved in his case. His explanation is private, and through it the defendant hopes to minimize the sanction to be imposed by the judge. But how offenders account for their behavior in nonjudicial settings is an open question, the answer to which may shed light on the perplexing ability of white-collar offenders to avoid being characterized as criminals even though they have been publicly convicted.

The major theme of the following discussion is that accounting for involvement in a white-collar offense is intimately involved with the social organization of the offense. The accounts developed by white-collar offenders are delimited by the type of offense committed, its mechanics, and its organizational context. They are further structured in that they must be constructed so as to defeat the conditions required for a successful degradation ceremony.

THE STUDY

This study is based primarily on interviews conducted with a sample of 30 convicted white-collar offenders. The interviews were supplemented by an examination of the files maintained on 80 white-collar offenders and by further interviews with federal probation officers, federal judges, Assistant U.S. Attorneys, and defense attorneys specializing in white-collar cases.

The sample of interviewed offenders was essentially self-selected. A letter which introduced the researcher and described the nature of the study was sent to most of the 80 offenders in the sample.[4] The letter indicated that the researcher was interested

---

[4] Some offenders whose files were examined were not available to be interviewed, because they were incarcerated at the time of the study.

in the subject's impressions of the way in which his case was handled and in the effect that conviction had on his self-image and life prospects.[5] Offenders were assured that their remarks would not be attributable to them as individuals. The proposed interviews would be open-ended and unstructured.

In light of the small and nonrandom nature of the sample, the results reported here must be viewed as provisional. There are no systematic differences between the offenders who agreed to be interviewed and those who did not in terms of their social and offense characteristics, but there is some likelihood that the interviewees differed psychologically or experientially from those who refused to participate.

The letter inviting participation in the study was sent from the Probation Office, and it is possible that some offenders viewed their participation as a way of ingratiating themselves with their respective probation officers. They also may have felt under some coercion to participate in the study. While these potential sources of bias cannot be completely ruled out, it is the researcher's impression that most of the interviewees agreed to participate because they welcomed an opportunity to express their views on the criminal justice system in a confidential and nonjudgmental forum.

In the interviews no attempt was made to challenge the explanations or rationalizations given by offenders regarding their offenses. Rather, offenders were encouraged to talk of themselves and their feelings regarding the case and they were allowed to focus on the aspects they considered to be most important. This approach was followed for two reasons: first, the sensitive nature of the subject matter under discussion did not permit the use of an interrogatory or inquisitorial style. The emotional trauma wrought by conviction was, indeed, evident in many of the interviews and, considering the voluntary nature of the interviews, to challenge the subjects seemed insensitive and unnecessary. Second, the goal of the study was not to determine how strong the rationalizations were, nor was it to bring about a "rehabilitative" awareness in the offender of the criminality of past acts. Rather, it was to determine how offenders account for their actions to themselves and to significant others, who it is assumed are unlikely to challenge or refute their explanations.

The Offenders

For the purposes of this study, white-collar offenders were those convicted of economic offenses committed through the use of indirection, fraud, or collusion (Shapiro, 1980). The offenses represented in the sample are those that are usually thought of as presumptively white-collar offenses, such as securities and exchange fraud, antitrust violations, embezzlement, false claims and statements, and tax violations. In terms of socioeconomic status, the sample ranges from a formerly successful practitioner of international law to a man currently self-employed as a seller of jewelry trinkets. For

---

[5] All of the offenders who consented to being interviewed were men.

some offenders, particularly licensed professionals and those employed in the public sector, conviction was accompanied by loss of occupation and other major changes in life-style. For others, such as businessmen and those employed in the private sector, conviction was not accompanied by collateral disabilities other than the expense and trauma of criminal justice processing (Benson, 1984).

Accounts

An account is a statement made to explain unanticipated or untoward behavior (Scott and Lyman, 1968). There are two general forms of accounts: (1) justifications, and (2) excuses. In a justification the actor admits responsibility for the act in question but denies its pejorative content. In an excuse the actor admits the act in question is wrong, but denies having full responsibility for it. Accounts are used to narrow the gap between expectation and behavior and to present the actor in a favorable light. They serve, that is, an exculpatory function. Related to the justification and the excuse is the apology. In an apology, the individual admits violating a rule, accepts the validity of the rule, and expresses embarrassment and anger at himself. The individual "splits himself into two parts, the part that is guilty of an offense and the part that disassociates itself from the delict and affirms a belief in the offended rule" (Goffman, 1972: 113).

Two perspectives are possible on the psychological status of accounts. They can be viewed as impression management techniques used by the offender to exonerate himself and to avoid being labeled a criminal. Alternatively, they can be viewed as indicators of the offender's cognitive structure—that is, of the way he interprets what he did. The present study cannot demonstrate conclusively which of these perspectives is more accurate. Given the obvious interest that offenders have in maintaining a noncriminal identity, the impression management perspective is perhaps more plausible in this instance. Nonetheless, it should be recognized that offenders probably engage in a process of self-persuasion in defining their situations. Accounts intended to shore up the offender's public identity may evolve into the offender's own view of himself and his offense. Regardless of which perspective is more appropriate, it can be suggested that the study of accounts has important implications for the field of criminology.

On the one hand, accounts relate to the techniques of neutralization identified by Sykes and Matza (1957) in their seminal article on juvenile delinquency. According to Sykes and Matza, before committing offenses juvenile delinquents use techniques of neutralization to relieve themselves of the duty to behave according to the norms. The study of neutralizations is important, therefore, in helping us to understand the individual and situational causes of crime. Whether white-collar offenders engage in a similar process before their offenses is not clear in all instances. One prominent theory of embezzlement hinges on this assumption (Cressey, 1953). Considering that almost by definition white-collar offenders are more strongly committed to the central normative structure, it is reasonable to assume that many of them go through elabo-rate neutralization processes prior to their offenses. The accounts developed after-wards may describe the process employed by the offender. In this manner, the study of accounts can provide a guide to micro-level analysis of the causal factors involved in a white-collar crime.

An account, however, is not a foolproof guide to an actor's intentions (Nettler, 1982: 15–17). It is important to distinguish between neutralizations that cause or allow an offense to be committed and accounts that are developed afterwards to excuse or justify it. By definition, an account is a linguistic act presented to or, more correctly, performed before an audience. It is an example of what Goffman (1959) has called impression management.

In giving an account, the offender is not talking to himself for the purpose of identifying reasons that allow the commission of an offense. Rather, he is addressing an audience and attempting to explain the offense while at the same time demon-strating an essential lack of personal criminality. To accomplish this feat, he must bring his actions into correspondence with the class of actions that is implicitly acceptable in his society. For this reason, accounts should not be thought of as solely individual inventions. Rather, they are invented by, as well as in, an historical and institutional context. This context delimits the range of superficially plausible justi-fications and excuses.

Corporate capitalism creates opportunities for particular forms of crime and at the same time creates, or makes plausible, certain types of justifications and mitiga-tions for engaging in crime. The diffusion of responsibility in corporations, for example, makes it plausible for an actor to either deny responsibility altogether or to partially excuse actions by claiming to have been working at the request of superiors. The widespread acceptance of such concepts as profit, growth, and free enterprise makes it plausible for an actor to argue that governmental regulations run counter to more basic societal values and goals. Criminal behavior can then be characterized as being in line with other higher laws of free enterprise (Denzin, 1977: 919). More generally, the idea, which seems to be at the core of capitalist economies, that society benefits most through the individual competitive strivings of its members, as opposed to the opposite notion that society benefits most through the submerging of individual goals in favor of group needs, would seem to provide a moral environment which facilitates the rationalization of criminal behavior. The idea of "just trying to get ahead" becomes an understandable and perhaps acceptable motive even when it occasionally leads to behavior that violates the law. A similar defense (or motive) would not seem to be possible in societies that do not promote individual material success as a desirable goal.

The study of accounts, therefore, can reveal how history and social structure make possible certain characterizations of events. This creates a moral environment conducive to crime in two ways. Convicted offenders can rationalize their behavior to themselves prior to engaging in crimes. After the discovery of an offender's involvement in criminal activity, he may be able to avoid the stigma of being labeled a criminal through the use of proper accounting practices.

Accounts are important, therefore, for three reasons. First, they shed light on neutralizations and vocabularies of motive and help one to understand the causes of crime at the individual and situational level. Second, as modes of impression management, they illuminate underlying assumptions about what constitutes culpable criminality versus acceptable illegalities. Finally, as Rothman and Gandossy (1982) have demonstrated, some white-collar offenders are more successful than others in minimizing the sanctions they receive by virtue of the sufficiency of their accounts. Thus, accounts may play an important and poorly understood role in the judicial process.

DENYING THE GUILTY MIND

Adjudication as a criminal is, to use Garfinkel's (1956) classic term, a degradation ceremony. The focus of this article is on how offenders attempt to defeat the success of this ceremony and deny their own criminality through the use of accounts. However, in the interest of showing in as much detail as possible all sides of the experience undergone by these offenders, it is necessary to treat first the guilt and inner anguish that is felt by many white-collar offenders even though they deny being criminals. This is best accomplished by beginning with a description of a unique feature of the prosecution of white-collar crimes.

In white-collar criminal cases, the issue is likely to be *why* something was done, rather than *who* did it (Edelhertz, 1970: 47). There is often relatively little disagreement as to what happened. In the words of one Assistant U.S. Attorney interviewed for the study:

> If you actually had a movie playing, neither side would dispute that a person moved in this way and handled this piece of paper, etc. What it comes down to is, did they have the criminal intent?

If the prosecution is to proceed past the investigatory stages, the prosecutor must infer from the pattern of events that conscious criminal intent was present and believe that sufficient evidence exists to convince a jury of this interpretation of the situation. As Katz (1979b: 445–446) has noted, making this inference can be difficult because of the way in which white-collar illegalities are integrated into ordinary occupational routines. Thus, prosecutors in conducting trials, grand jury hearings, or plea negotiations spend a great deal of effort establishing that the defendant did indeed have the necessary criminal intent. By concentrating on the offender's motives, the prosecutor attacks the very essence of the white-collar offender's public and personal image as an upstanding member of the community. The offender is portrayed as someone with a guilty mind.

Not surprisingly, therefore, the most consistent and recurrent pattern in the interviews, though not present in all of them, was denial of criminal intent, as opposed to the outright denial of any criminal behavior whatsoever. Most offenders acknowledged that their behavior probably could be construed as falling within the conduct proscribed by statute, but they uniformly denied that their actions were motivated by a guilty mind. This is not to say, however, that offenders *felt* no guilt or shame as a result of conviction. On the contrary, indictment, prosecution, and conviction provoke a variety of emotions among offenders.

The enormous reality of the offender's lived emotion (Denzin, 1984) in admitting guilt is perhaps best illustrated by one offender's description of his feelings during the hearing at which he pled guilty.

> You know (the plea's) what really hurt. I didn't even know I had feet. I felt numb. My head was just floating. There was no feeling, except a state of suspended animation.... For a brief moment, I almost hesitated. I almost said not guilty. If I had been alone, I would have fought, but my family....

The traumatic nature of this moment lies, in part, in the offender's feeling that only one aspect of his life is being considered. From the offender's point of view his crime represents only one small part of his life. It does not typify his inner self, and to judge him solely on the basis of this one event seems an atrocious injustice to the offender.

For some the memory of the event is so painful that they want to obliterate it entirely, as the two following quotations illustrate.

> I want quiet. I want to forget. I want to cut with the past.

> I've already divorced myself from the problem. I don't even want to hear the names of certain people ever again. It brings me pain.

For others, rage rather than embarrassment seemed to be the dominant emotion.

> I never really felt any embarrassment over the whole thing. I felt rage and it wasn't false or self-serving. It was really (something) to see this thing in action and recognize what the whole legal system has come to through its development, and the abuse of the grand jury system and the abuse of the indictment system....

The role of the news media in the process of punishment and stigmatization should not be overlooked. All offenders whose cases were reported on by the news media were either embarrassed or embittered or both by the public exposure.

> The only one I am bitter at is the newspapers, as many people are. They are unfair because you can't get even. They can say things that are untrue, and let me say this to you. They wrote an article on me that was so blasphemous, that was so horrible. They painted me as an insidious, miserable creature, wringing out the last penny....

Offenders whose cases were not reported on by the news media expressed relief at having avoided that kind of embarrassment, sometimes saying that greater publicity would have been worse than any sentence they could have received.

In court, defense lawyers are fond of presenting white-collar offenders as having suffered enough by virtue of the humiliation of public adjudication as criminals. On the other hand, prosecutors present them as cavalier individuals who arrogantly ignore the law and brush off its weak efforts to stigmatize them as criminals. Neither of these stereotypes is entirely accurate. The subjective effects of conviction on white-collar offenders are varied and complex. One suspects that this is true of all offenders, not only white-collar offenders.

The emotional responses of offenders to conviction have not been the subject of extensive research. However, insofar as an individual's emotional response to adjudication may influence the deterrent or crime-reinforcing impact of punishment on him or her, further study might reveal why some offenders stop their criminal behavior while others go on to careers in crime (Casper, 1978: 80).

Although the offenders displayed a variety of different emotions with respect to their experiences, they were nearly unanimous in denying basic criminality. To see how white-collar offenders justify and excuse their crimes, we turn to their accounts. The small number of cases rules out the use of any elaborate classification techniques. Nonetheless, it is useful to group offenders by offense when presenting their interpretations.

Antitrust Violators

Four of the offenders had been convicted of antitrust violations, all in the same case involving the building and contracting industry. Four major themes characterized their accounts. First, antitrust offenders focused on the everyday character and historical continuity of their offenses.

> It was a way of doing business before we even got into the business. So it was like why do you brush your teeth in the morning or something. . . . It was part of the everyday. . . . It was a method of survival.

The offenders argued that they were merely following established and necessary industry practices. These practices were presented as being necessary for the well-being of the industry as a whole, not to mention their own companies. Further, they argued that cooperation among competitors was either allowed or actively promoted by the government in other industries and professions.

The second theme emphasized by the offenders was the characterization of their actions as blameless. They admitted talking to competitors and admitted submitting intentionally noncompetitive bids. However, they presented these practices as being done not for the purpose of rigging prices nor to make exorbitant profits. Rather, the everyday practices of the industry required them to occasionally submit bids on projects they really did not want to have. To avoid the effort and expense of preparing full-fledged bids, they would call a competitor to get a price to use. Such a situation might arise, for example, when a company already had enough work for the time being, but was asked by a valued customer to submit a bid anyway.

> All you want to do is show a bid, so that in some cases it was for as small a reason as getting your deposit back on the plans and specs. So you just simply have no interest in getting the job and just call to see if you can find someone to give you a price to use, so that you didn't have to go through the expense of an entire bid preparation. Now that is looked on very unfavorably, and it is a technical violation, but it was strictly an opportunity to keep your name in front of a desired customer. Or you may find yourself in a situation where somebody is doing work for a customer, has done work for many, many years and is totally acceptable, totally fair. There is no problem. But suddenly they (the customer) get an idea that they ought to have a few tentative figures, and you're called in, and you are in a moral dilemma. There's really no reason for you to attempt to compete in that circumstance. And so there was a way to back out.

Managed in this way, an action that appears on the surface to be a straightforward and conscious violation of antitrust regulations becomes merely a harmless business practice that happens to be a "technical violation." The offender can then refer to his personal history to verify his claim that, despite technical violations, he is in reality a law-abiding person. In the words of one offender, "Having been in the business for 33 years, you don't just automatically become a criminal overnight."

Third, offenders were very critical of the motives and tactics of prosecutors. Prosecutors were accused of being motivated solely by the opportunity for personal advancement presented by winning a big case. Further, they were accused of employing prosecution selectively and using tactics that allowed the most culpable offenders to go free. The Department of Justice was painted as using antitrust prosecutions for political purposes.

The fourth theme emphasized by the antitrust offenders involved a comparison between their crimes and the crimes of street criminals. Antitrust offenses differ in their mechanics from street crimes in that they are not committed in one place and at one time. Rather, they are spatially and temporally diffuse and are intermingled with legitimate behavior. In addition, the victims of antitrust offenses tend not to be identifiable individuals, as is the case with most street crimes. These characteristics are used by antitrust violators to contrast their own behavior with that of common stereotypes of criminality. Real crimes are pictured as discrete events that have beginnings and ends and involve individuals who directly and purposely victimize someone else in a particular place and at a particular time.

> It certainly wasn't a premeditated type of thing in our cases as far as I can see.... To me it's different than ___ and I sitting down and we plan, well, we're going to rob this bank tomorrow and premeditatedly go in there.... That wasn't the case at all.... It wasn't like sitting down and planning I'm going to rob this bank type of thing.... It was just a common everyday way of doing business and surviving.

A consistent thread running through all of the interviews was the necessity for antitrust-like practices, given the realities of the business world. Offenders seemed to define the situation in such a manner that two sets of rules could be seen to apply. On the one hand, there are the legislatively determined rules—laws—which govern how one is to conduct one's business affairs. On the other hand, there is a higher set of rules based on the concepts of profit and survival, which are taken to define what it means to be in business in a capitalistic society. These rules do not just regulate behavior; rather, they constitute or create the behavior in question. If one is not trying to make a profit or trying to keep one's business going, then one is not really "in business." Following Searle (1969: 33–41), the former type of rule can be called a regulative rule and the latter type a constitutive rule. In certain situations, one may have to violate a regulative rule in order to conform to the more basic constitutive rule of the activity in which one is engaged.

This point can best be illustrated through the use of an analogy involving competitive games. Trying to win is a constitutive rule of competitive games in the sense that if one is not trying to win, one is not really playing the game. In competitive games, situations may arise where a player deliberately breaks the rules even though he knows or expects he will be caught. In the game of basketball, for example, a player may deliberately foul an opponent to prevent him from making a sure basket. In this instance, one would understand that the fouler was trying to win by gambling that the opponent would not make the free throws. The player violates the rule against fouling in order to follow the higher rule of trying to win.

Trying to make a profit or survive in business can be thought of as a constitutive rule of capitalist economies. The laws that govern *how* one is allowed to make a profit are regulative rules, which can understandably be subordinated to the rules of trying to survive and profit. From the offender's point of view, he is doing what businessmen in our society are supposed to do—that is, stay in business and make a profit. Thus, an individual who violates society's laws or regulations in certain situations may actually conceive of himself as thereby acting more in accord with the central ethos of his society than if he had been a strict observer of its law. One might suggest, following Denzin (1977), that for businessmen in the building and contracting industry, an informal structure exists below the articulated legal structure, one which frequently supersedes the legal structure. The informal structure may define as moral and "legal" certain actions that the formal legal structure defines as immoral and "illegal."

Tax Violators

Six of the offenders interviewed were convicted of income tax violations. Like antitrust violators, tax violators can rely upon the complexity of the tax laws and an historical tradition in which cheating on taxes is not really criminal. Tax offenders would claim that everybody cheats somehow on their taxes and present themselves as victims of an unlucky break, because they got caught.

> Everybody cheats on their income tax, 95% of the people. Even if it's for ten dollars it's the same principle. I didn't cheat. I just didn't know how to report it.

The widespread belief that cheating on taxes is endemic helps to lend credence to the offender's claim to have been singled out and to be no more guilty than most people.

Tax offenders were more likely to have acted as individuals rather than as part of a group and, as a result, were more prone to account for their offenses by referring to them as either mistakes or the product of special circumstances. Violations were presented as simple errors which resulted from ignorance and poor recordkeeping. Deliberate intention to steal from the government for personal benefit was denied.

> I didn't take the money. I have no bank account to show for all this money, where all this money is at that I was supposed to have. They never found the money, ever. There is no Swiss bank account, believe me.

> My records were strictly one big mess. That's all it was. If only I had an accountant, this wouldn't even of happened. No way in God's creation would this ever have happened.

Other offenders would justify their actions by admitting that they were wrong while painting their motives as altruistic rather than criminal. Criminality was denied because they did not set out to deliberately cheat the government for their own personal gain. Like the antitrust offenders discussed above, one tax violator distinguished between his own crime and the crimes of real criminals.

> I'm not a criminal. That is, I'm not a criminal from the standpoint of taking a gun and doing this and that. I'm a criminal from the standpoint of making a mistake, a serious mistake. . . . The thing that really got me involved in it is my feeling for the employees here, certain employees that are my right hand. In order to save them a certain amount of taxes and things like that, I'd extend money to them in cash, and the money came from these sources that I took it from. You know, cash sales and things of that nature, but practically all of it was turned over to the employees, because of my feeling for them.

All of the tax violators pointed out that they had no intention of deliberately victimizing the government. None of them denied the legitimacy of the tax laws, nor did they claim that they cheated because the government is not representative of the people (Conklin, 1977: 99). Rather, as a result of ignorance or for altruistic reasons, they made decisions which turned out to be criminal when viewed from the perspective of the law. While they acknowledged the technical criminality of their actions, they tried to show that what they did was not criminally motivated.

Violations of Financial Trust

Four offenders were involved in violations of financial trust. Three were bank officers who embezzled or misapplied funds, and the fourth was a union official who embezzled from a union pension fund. Perhaps because embezzlement is one crime in this sample that can be considered *mala in se*,[6] these offenders were much more forthright about their crimes. Like the other offenders, the embezzlers would not go so far as to say "I am a criminal," but they did say "What I did was wrong, was criminal, and I knew it was." Thus, the embezzlers were unusual in that they explicitly admitted responsibility for their crimes. Two of the offenders clearly fit Cressey's scheme as persons with financial problems who used their positions to convert other people's money to their own use.

Unlike tax evasion, which can be excused by reference to the complex nature of tax regulations or antitrust violations, which can be justified as for the good of the organization as a whole, embezzlement requires deliberate action on the part of the offender and is almost inevitably committed for personal reasons. The crime of embezzlement, therefore, cannot be accounted for by using the same techniques that tax violators or antitrust violators do. The act itself can only be explained by showing that one was under extraordinary circumstances which explain one's uncharacteristic behavior. Three of the offenders referred explicitly to extraordinary circumstances and presented the offense as an aberration in their life history. For example, one offender described his situation in this manner:

> As a kid, I never even—you know kids will sometimes shoplift from the dime store—I never even did that. I had never stolen a thing in my life and that was what was so unbelieveable about the whole thing, but there were some psychological and personal questions that I wasn't dealing with very well. I wasn't terribly happily married. I was married to a very strong-willed woman and it just wasn't working out.

The offender in this instance goes on to explain how, in an effort to impress his wife, he lived beyond his means and fell into debt.

A structural characteristic of embezzlement also helps the offender demonstrate his essential lack of criminality. Embezzlement is integrated into ordinary occupational routines. The illegal action does not stand out clearly against the surrounding set of legal actions. Rather, there is a high degree of surface correspondence between legal and illegal behavior. To maintain this correspondence, the offender must exercise some restraint when committing his crime. The embezzler must be discreet in his stealing; he cannot take all of the money available to him without at the same time revealing the crime. Once exposed, the offender can point to this restraint on his part as evidence that he is not really a criminal. That is, he can compare what happened with what could have happened in order to show how much more serious the offense could have been if he was really a criminal at heart.

> What I could have done if I had truly had a devious criminal mind and perhaps if I had been a little smarter—and I am not saying that with any degree of pride or any degree of modesty whatever, [as] it's being smarter in a bad, an evil way—I could have pulled this off on a grander scale and I might still be doing it.

---

[6] Latin: inherently wrong. [Ed.]

Even though the offender is forthright about admitting his guilt, he makes a distinction between himself and someone with a truly "devious criminal mind."

Contrary to Cressey's (1953: 57–66) findings, none of the embezzlers claimed that their offenses were justified because they were underpaid or badly treated by their employers. Rather, attention was focused on the unusual circumstances surrounding the offense and its atypical character when compared to the rest of the offender's life. This strategy is for the most part determined by the mechanics and organizational format of the offense itself. Embezzlement occurs within the organization but not for the organization. It cannot be committed accidentally or out of ignorance. It can be accounted for only by showing that the actor "was not himself" at the time of the offense or was under such extraordinary circumstances that embezzlement was an understandable response to an unfortunate situation. This may explain the finding that embezzlers tend to produce accounts that are viewed as more sufficient by the justice system than those produced by other offenders (Rothman and Gandossy, 1982). The only plausible option open to a convicted embezzler trying to explain his offense is to admit responsibility while justifying the action, an approach that apparently strikes a responsive chord with judges.

Fraud and False Statements

Ten offenders were convicted of some form of fraud or false statements charge. Unlike embezzlers, tax violators, or antitrust violators, these offenders were much more likely to deny committing any crime at all. Seven of the ten claimed that they, personally, were innocent of any crime, although each admitted that fraud had occurred. Typically, they claimed to have been set up by associates and to have been wrongfully convicted by the U.S. Attorney handling the case. One might call this the scapegoat strategy. Rather than admitting technical wrongdoing and then justifying or excusing it, the offender attempts to paint himself as a victim by shifting the blame entirely to another party. Prosecutors were presented as being either ignorant or politically motivated.

The outright denial of any crime whatsoever is unusual compared to the other types of offenders studied here. It may result from the nature of the crime of fraud. By definition, fraud involves a conscious attempt on the part of one or more persons to mislead others. While it is theoretically possible to accidentally violate the antitrust and tax laws, or to violate them for altruistic reasons, it is difficult to imagine how one could accidentally mislead someone else for his or her own good. Furthermore, in many instances, fraud is an aggressively acquisitive crime. The offender develops a scheme to bilk other people out of money or property, and does this not because of some personal problem but because the scheme is an easy way to get rich. Stock swindles, fraudulent loan scams, and so on are often so large and complicated that they cannot possibly be excused as foolish and desperate solutions to personal problems. Thus, those involved in large-scale frauds do not have the option open to most embezzlers of presenting themselves as persons responding defensively to difficult personal circumstances.

Furthermore, because fraud involves a deliberate attempt to mislead another, the offender who fails to remove himself from the scheme runs the risk of being shown to have a guilty mind. That is, he is shown to possess the most essential element of modern conceptions of criminality: an intent to harm another. His inner self would in this case be exposed as something other than what it has been presented as, and all of his previous actions would be subject to reinterpretation in light of this new perspective. For this reason, defrauders are most prone to denying any crime at all. The cooperative and conspiratorial nature of many fraudulent schemes makes it possible to put the blame on someone else and to present oneself as a scapegoat. Typically, this is done by claiming to have been duped by others.

Two illustrations of this strategy are presented below.

> I figured I wasn't guilty, so it wouldn't be that hard to disprove it, until, as I say, I went to court and all of a sudden they start bringing in these guys out of the woodwork implicating me that I never saw. Lot of it could be proved that I never saw.

> Inwardly, I personally felt that the only crime that I committed was not telling on these guys. Not that I deliberately, intentionally committed a crime against the system. My only crime was that I should have had the guts to tell on these guys, what they were doing, rather than putting up with it and then trying to gradually get out of the system without hurting them or without them thinking I was going to snitch on them.

Of the three offenders who admitted committing crimes, two acted alone and the third acted with only one other person. Their accounts were similar to the others presented earlier and tended to focus on either the harmless nature of their violations or on the unusual circumstances that drove them to commit their crimes. One claimed that his violations were only technical and that no one besides himself had been harmed.

> First of all, no money was stolen or anything of that nature. The bank didn't lose any money. . . . What I did was a technical violation. I made a mistake. There's no question about that, but the bank lost no money.

Another offender who directly admitted his guilt was involved in a check-kiting scheme. In a manner similar to embezzlers, he argued that his actions were motivated by exceptional circumstances.

> I was faced with the choice of all of a sudden, and I mean now, closing the doors or doing something else to keep that business open. . . . I'm not going to tell you that this wouldn't have happened if I'd had time to think it over, because I think it probably would have. You're sitting there with a dying patient. You are going to try to keep him alive.

In the other fraud cases more individuals were involved, and it was possible and perhaps necessary for each offender to claim that he was not really the culprit.

DISCUSSION: OFFENSES, ACCOUNTS, AND DEGRADATION CEREMONIES

The investigation, prosecution, and conviction of a white-collar offender involves him in a very undesirable status passage (Glaser and Strauss, 1971). The entire process can be viewed as a long and drawn-out degradation ceremony with the prosecutor as the chief denouncer and the offender's family and friends as the chief witnesses. The offender is moved from the status of law-abiding citizen to that of convicted felon. Accounts are developed to defeat the process of identity transformation that is the object of a degradation ceremony. They represent the offender's attempt to diminish the effect of his legal transformation and to prevent its becoming a publicly validated label. It can be suggested that the accounts developed by white-collar offenders take the forms that they do for two reasons: (1) the forms are required to defeat the success of the degradation ceremony, and (2) the specific forms used are the ones available given the mechanics, history, and organizational context of the offenses.

Three general patterns in accounting strategies stand out in the data. Each can be characterized by the subject matter on which it focuses: the event (offense), the perpetrator (offender), or the denouncer (prosecutor). These are the natural subjects of accounts in that to be successful, a degradation ceremony requires each of these elements to be presented in a particular manner (Garfinkel, 1956). If an account giver can undermine the presentation of one or more of the elements, then the effect of the ceremony can be reduced. Although there are overlaps in the accounting strategies used by the various types of offenders, and while any given offender may use more than one strategy, it appears that accounting strategies and offenses correlate.

Event

In order for a degradation ceremony to be successful, the event must be shown to be out of the ordinary. It must be revealed as obviously and unquestionably profane. Further, the event must be indicative of a pattern of behavior that is the opposite of that expected of the normal citizen. When an account focuses on the event, therefore, the object is to remove the pejorative content from the behavior in question. Rather than being exposed as something out of the ordinary, its similarity to accepted and routine practices must be emphasized. If this option is not available, then the account must portray the event as an aberration and not representative of typical behavior patterns.

Antitrust violators focus on the event itself and present it as a normal, everyday practice. In so doing, they are in essence attempting to show that the offense is not "out of the ordinary." Rather, it is normal and so is the offender. Similarly, tax violators also focus on the widespread incidence of tax violations. A practice that is widespread can hardly be considered as out of the ordinary.

In addition to historical tradition, antitrust offenders also refer to organizational loyalty and a complex business environment. These tactics have the effect of showing that the offense cannot be separated from its environment and made to stand out as an inherently and unquestionably profane event. It is presented in such a manner that its dialectical counterpart, to use Garfinkel's terminology, is not immediately obvious. In one sense, this attempted normalization has not succeeded. The offender has, after all, been convicted. But, in a wider societal context, it may have been successful. To the extent that white-collar offenders are not ostracized by family, friends, and business associates and to the extent that they can continue in their occupational careers, they have maintained their normalcy.

The embezzler faces a different problem when confronted with proof of his offense. He cannot refer to its routine and everyday character or to its widespread prevalence. Rather, the offense must be shown to be an aberration from his regular behavior patterns, a unique, one-time-only mistake. This approach leads quite naturally to his role as perpetrator.

Perpetrator

Perpetrators must be characterized in much the same manner as events. That is, the true character of the perpetrator must be revealed as out of the ordinary and unquestionably profane. Most importantly, the perpetrator must be presented as all of one piece. The multifaceted and ambiguous nature of his personality must be denied and any sense of chance or accident must be made inconceivable. Thus, when the perpetrator is the subject of the account, the account giver must show that no matter how the event is eventually characterized, it is not indicative of his true character. That is, the account giver must separate himself from the offense and emphasize its unique character. Above all, the offender must show that he is not out of the ordinary, but rather is an understandable individual. This strategy is plausibly used by tax violators and embezzlers.

Tax violators are prone to focus on themselves as inadvertent perpetrators. Their crimes are presented as mistakes or oversights and, most importantly, as not indicative of their true identity.

> I'm sure you must have seen my background. I was in government service. I've had federal army service for 33 years, and my record is not only excellent but outstanding in all these particular fields. . . . I think in all my years I made one mistake and this was the mistake I made.

If an offender can show that his offense was an aberration, regardless of whether it is the result of ignorance, confusion, or bad judgment, he can avoid being labeled a criminal. Antitrust violators cannot really present their offenses as wholly uncharacteristic aberrations, but they can emphasize their confusion over what was really criminal and their ignorance of the law.

Embezzlers also focus on their role as perpetrators rather than attempting to justify their offenses. But, unlike tax violators, they are forthright in admitting responsibility for their crimes. In a sense, they have no other option because the crime certainly cannot be committed by accident or to help the organization. Thus, the embezzler is left with showing that he was not himself when he committed the offense. He must refer to special circumstances or extraordinary pressures and argue that his offense was out of character. Set in this context, the crime is revealed as an aberration, a momentary lapse, or insignificant when compared to an otherwise exemplary and impeccable moral career.

The strategy of context setting is the reverse of the process of retrospective interpretation through which deviant statuses are conferred on less powerful individuals, wherein events are reinterpreted to show how they constitute a pattern of deviance (Goffman, 1961: 151–155; Schur, 1971: 52–56; Kitsuse, 1962; Lofland, 1966: 155–158). Embezzlers and other white-collar offenders must show that the offense is not part of a pattern. It must be presented as a one-time-only break from the real pattern of the offender's life. The lack of a prior criminal record and a personal history of accomplishment greatly facilitates the typical white-collar offender's ability to make these points and have them carry a modicum of legitimacy. Further, modern penological theory with its emphasis on taking into account the totality of circumstances surrounding the offender and offense provides an ideological ground for this strategy. If environmental conditions are to be considered when it comes to evaluating a street criminal, then certainly it is reasonable for a white-collar offender to argue that the many positive features of his personal history should be considered when judgments of him are to be made.

There is some evidence that an offender's ability to contrast the crime with the rest of his life and to show that it is an aberration in an otherwise impeccable life does have a mitigating effect on societal reactions. Wheeler, Weisburd, and Bode (1982), in a study of the sentencing of white-collar offenders, found that those who came from impeccable backgrounds were less likely to be incarcerated or were incarcerated for shorter periods of time than those from less impeccable backgrounds (see also Mann, Wheeler, and Sarat, 1980). The effect of impeccability on sanctions was independent and opposite that of social status. White-collar offenders are, of course, much more likely to have impeccable backgrounds than are common offenders and thus much better equipped to show that their offenses are aberrations, rather than instances in a pattern.

Denouncer

The denouncer must not be seen as being personally involved in the case. That is, he must display no self-interest in the outcome. Rather, he must present himself as a representative of sacred values and claim to speak for them for the public good. Accounts focused on the denouncer must show that he does not speak for important and sacred values, but rather is motivated by personal interest. In this sense, condemning the condemners is not just sour grapes. It is, instead, an attack upon the legitimacy of the role occupied by the denouncer.

Antitrust offenders and those convicted of fraud were most prone to condemn their condemners. They claimed that the prosecutors assigned to their cases were motivated by personal interest rather than a desire to defend social or legal values, and that they were singled out for political or other reasons that had nothing to do with the harmfulness of their behavior. Such a strategy makes sense in that a denouncer must never be seen as being personally interested in the outcome of the ceremony. He must present himself as speaking only for the group's values and not for any other purpose.

The proactive nature of many white-collar investigations may facilitate the undermining of the denouncer's status as a personally disinterested public servant. Unlike street crimes, the prosecutor is often involved in the early stages of investigation for many white-collar offenses (Katz, 1979b). In their accounts, offenders present the prosecutor's active role in directing the investigation as evidence that he is personally committed to convicting somebody for something. The practice of "focusing" on a particular industry or segment of the economy is recast by offenders as evidence that they, not the offense itself, have been the targets of the judicial system and thus that their behavior is not inherently contrary to unquestionable values. In addition, the checkered history of antitrust litigation is available to antitrust violators. As Nader and Green (1972) have shown, the prosecution of antitrust offenses waxes and wanes with changes in presidential administrations and with the political fortunes of big business. The apparent fluctuation in the status of behavior that violates antitrust law becomes itself an accounting resource in that the offender can argue that his behavior has not been regarded as inherently or even customarily wrong.

Complete Denial

Complete denial of all wrongdoing was rare. Those convicted of fraud were more likely than the other offenders to completely deny committing any crime at all. This may result from the structure of the offense of fraud. The complex and conspiratorial nature of fraud undermines any attempt to present the offense as a response to desperate circumstances. In defrauding another, an offender pretends he is trustworthy when, in fact, he is not. In addition, by means of deceit, he induces others to act contrary to their own best interests. In this sense fraud is a more aggressive crime than embezzlement. Once the fact of fraud is proven, it is difficult for the offender to admit his role in it while attempting to present himself as basically noncriminal. The only option in these situations is to deny involvement altogether, present oneself as a scapegoat, and shift the blame to another party.

SUMMARY AND IMPLICATIONS

This study of convicted white-collar offenders has examined their accounts of their crimes. In particular, attention was given to the techniques used by offenders to deny their criminality and to maintain a legitimate persona. Accounts appear to be structured by the nature of the offense, its organizational format and history, and by the requirement that they undermine the conditions of successful degradation ceremonies. The most consistent and strongly emphasized theme manifested in the interviews was the denial of criminal intent.

In effect, offenders attempt to adjust the normative lens through which their offenses are viewed by society.[7] Societal reaction to crimes and criminals varies according to many factors. Although there is no clear-cut consensus on the number and relative importance of factors, it can be assumed that two elements of significance are (1) the seriousness of the offense, and (2) the blameworthiness of the offender. Any offender interested in avoiding being labeled a criminal must be able to minimize the blameworthiness and seriousness of his actions to a degree such that the label "criminal" will be regarded as inappropriate.

It can be suggested that the presentability of an offense may play an important role in an offender's decision to commit that offense. That is, for individuals interested in maintaining a noncriminal identity, offenses that appear, or can be made to appear, less serious and less blameworthy will be more attractive than those that cannot be so presented. White-collar crimes are often structured or organizationally situated such that they are more malleable in this regard than traditional crimes. Although it would be premature to propose a theory of white-collar crime on the basis of the accounts studied here, some preliminary observations can be made within the scheme suggested above.

Seriousness

The partial legitimacy of the outcomes of some white-collar crimes seems to play an important role in the offender's minimization of seriousness. Some antitrust offenses, tax violations, and false statements made to lending institutions have as their outcomes more than just illegal gain for the perpetrators. They may also shore up a failing business or provide stability in employment. While defrauding the Medicaid system, a doctor or dentist may also be providing at least some much-needed services for the poor. The harm experienced by the victim or victims is balanced against the benefits derived by other uninvolved parties, such as employees and family. The congruence of legitimacy and illegitimacy that characterizes the commission of white-collar and

---

[7] The idea of a "normative lens" and much of the following discussion is indebted to a paper presented at an annual meeting of the American Society of Criminology by Wheeler (1984).

corporate crimes (Clinard and Quinney, 1973) may be reproduced in the final products of those crimes and in the justifications presented by offenders.

A belief in widespread illegality was frequently expressed in the interviews. It seemed to be assumed that everybody is unscrupulous in one way or another. This fosters a callousness of attitude with regard to criminal behavior (Denzin, 1977). Criminal behavior is seen as acceptable and necessary for survival in the business world. This belief leads to the view that certain types of law violations, since they are normal, are not really serious crimes, which provides a blanket excuse for illegal behavior.

The belief in widespread illegality extends beyond the legitimate business world to society at large, which offenders seem to assume is at the mercy of rampant and unpunished street criminality. The lack of identifiable individual victims has been suggested as one of the reasons for the lack of societal concern with white-collar criminality. This characteristic of white-collar offenses may also be used by offenders before they commit their crimes. That is, the lack of individual victims may help the offender in using the familiar neutralization techniques of denying the victim and the harm.

Blameworthiness

The complexity of the laws and regulations governing the business world seems to facilitate relieving the offender's sense of blameworthiness. Crimes committed out of ignorance or inattention to detail are less offensive to the social conscience than those deliberately committed. Unlike the common street crimes, it is possible to accidentally violate laws that govern the conduct of businesses, professions, and industries. This means that the motives underlying conduct cannot automatically be inferred from the conduct itself. An offense that would be considered blameworthy if committed knowingly may be excusable, or at least understandable, if committed out of ignorance. Complexity gives rise to an ambiguity in the connection between the act and its motive. This may allow offenders to persuade themselves and others that the motive was not really criminal, so therefore the act was not really a crime.

Such a process may even work in advance of the crime when offenders maintain a concerted ignorance of the law or of the activities of subordinates. Katz (1979a) has argued that individuals involved in organizational crimes are frequently aware that there is a chance that the crime will eventually come to light. Yet, even though discovery is a possibility, offenders may nonetheless choose to participate provided that they can construct anticipatory defenses that will allow them to eventually deny blameworthiness. Many features of corporate organization facilitate the building of these "metaphysical escapes" (Katz, 1979a). In other words, offenders may purposely attempt to structure crimes so that the connection between act and motive remains ambiguous and deniable.

Individuals who commit crimes outside an organizational context or who act against organizations (embezzlers) may attempt to reduce their blameworthiness by setting the crime within the context of an otherwise impeccable life. If a crime can be shown to be an aberration, then its importance as an indicator of the offender's true character is dramatically reduced. His or her personality can be shown to have both good and bad points with the good outnumbering the bad. The obvious inconsistency of the offender's conviction vis-a-vis the rest of his life may be handled by family, friends, and perhaps society at large by denying the implications of the offender's actions in order to maintain a consistent and favorable attitude toward him (Geis, 1982: 97).

As with the use of concerted ignorance, the process of setting the crime within a context of impeccability may be used by offenders prior to the illegal act as a neutralization technique. A lifetime of socially acceptable and desirable behavior in one arena is used to excuse an occasional indiscretion in another.

What needs to be determined is how effective these strategies are in helping the offender avoid stigmatization as a criminal—that is, avoid being thought of and treated like a criminal by others. If certain classes of offenders can commit crimes, be convicted, and yet still, through the use of appropriate accounting strategies, avoid being labeled as criminals, then one of the primary functions of the criminal law and the criminal justice system—the symbolic separation of the offender from the community—is negated. A moral environment is thereby perpetuated in which the symbolic consequences of criminal behavior for some offenders can largely be ignored.

REFERENCES

Becker, Howard S. 1963. Outsiders. New York: Free Press.

Benson, Michael. 1984. The fall from grace: Loss of occupational status among white-collar offenders. Criminology 22: 573–593.

Casper, Jonathan D. 1978. Criminal Courts: The Defendant's Perspective. Washington, D.C.: U.S. Department of Justice.

Clinard, Marshall B. and Richard Quinney. 1973. Criminal Behavior Systems: A Typology. New York: Holt, Rinehart, and Winston.

Clinard, Marshall B. and Peter C. Yeager. 1978. Corporate crime: Issues in research. Criminology 16: 255–272.

Conklin, John E. 1977. Illegal But Not Criminal: Business Crime in America. Englewood Cliffs, NJ: Prentice-Hall.

Cressey, Donald. 1953. Other People's Money. New York: Free Press.

Denzin, Norman K. 1977. Notes on the criminogenic hypothesis: A case study of the American liquor industry. American Sociological Review 42: 905–920.

—— 1984. On Understanding Emotion. San Francisco: Jossey-Bass.

Edelhertz, Herbert. 1970. The Nature, Impact, and Prosecution of White Collar Crime. Washington, D.C.: U.S. Government Printing Office.

Fisse, Brent and John Braithwaite. 1983. The Impact of Publicity on Corporate Offenders. Albany, NY: State University of New York.

Garfinkel, Harold. 1956. Conditions of successful degradation ceremonies. American Journal of Sociology 61: 420–424.

Geis, Gilbert. 1967. The heavy electrical equipment antitrust cases of 1961. In Gilbert Geis and Robert Meier (eds.), White Collar Crime. New York: Free Press.

——— 1982. On White-Collar Crime. Lexington, MA: Lexington.

Glaser, Barney G. and Anselm L. Strauss. 1971. Status Passage. Chicago: Aldine.

Goffman, Erving. 1959. The Presentation of Self in Everyday Life. Garden City, NY: Anchor.

——— 1961. Asylums. Garden City, NY: Anchor.

——— 1972. Relations in Public. New York: Harper Colophon.

Katz, Jack. 1979a. Concerted ignorance: The social construction of cover-up. Urban Life 8: 295–316.

——— 1979b. Legality and equality: Plea bargaining in the prosecution of white-collar crimes. Law and Society Review 13: 431–460.

Kitsuse, John. 1962. Societal reaction to deviant behavior. Social Problems 9: 247–256.

Lofland, John. 1966. Deviance and Identity. Englewood Cliffs, NJ: Prentice-Hall.

Mann, Kenneth, Stanton Wheeler, and Austin Sarat. 1980. Sentencing the white-collar offender. American Criminal Law Review 17: 479–500.

Matza, David. 1969. Becoming Deviant. Englewood Cliffs, NJ: Prentice-Hall.

Meier, Robert and Gilbert Geis. 1982. The psychology of the white-collar offender. In Gilbert Geis (ed.), On White-Collar Crime. Lexington, MA: Lexington.

Nader, Ralph and Mark Green. 1972. Coddling the corporations: Crime in the suites. New Republic 166: 17–21.

Naughton, James M., John Crewdson, Ben Franklin, Christopher Lydon, and Agie Solpukas. 1977. How Agnew bartered his office to keep from going to jail. In Gilbert Geis and Robert F. Meier (eds.), White-Collar Crime. New York: Free Press.

Nettler, Gwynn. 1982. Explaining Criminals. Cincinnati, OH: Anderson.

Rothman, Martin and Robert F. Gandossy. 1982. Sad tales: The accounts of white-collar defendants and the decision to sanction. Pacific Sociological Review 4: 449–473.

Schur, Edwin. 1971. Labelling Deviant Behavior. New York: Harper and Row.

Scott, Marvin B. and Stanford M. Lyman. 1968. Accounts. American Sociological Review 33: 46–62.

Shapiro, Susan P. 1980. Thinking About White-Collar Crime: Matters of Conceptualization and Research. Washington, D.C.: U.S. Government Printing Office.

Searle, John R. 1969. Speech Acts. Cambridge: Cambridge University Press.

Sutherland, Edwin H. 1949. White Collar Crime. New York: Dryden.

Sykes, Gresham and David Matza. 1957. Techniques of neutralization: A theory of delinquency. American Sociological Review 22: 664–670.

Wheeler, Stanton. 1984. Sitting in judgment: Judicial perspectives on sentencing of white-collar offenders. Presented at the annual meeting of the American Society of Criminology.

Wheeler, Stanton, David Weisburd, and Nancy Bode. 1982. Sentencing the white-collar offender: Rhetoric and reality. American Sociological Review 47: 641–659.

STUDY QUESTIONS

1. What does the author mean by constitutive rules and regulative rules?

2. How did the tax violators justify their behavior?

3. What is the difference between tax violations and the violation of financial trust in relation to criminal motivation?

4. Use the FBI's website (www.fbi.gov) to learn more about **white-collar crime**. Pick one white-collar crime and share some interesting facts you learn about the crime, including information about the crime's perpetrators and effects.

ANNETTE LAREAU

Invisible Inequality: Social Class and Childrearing in Black Families and White Families

W ith few exceptions, parents love their children and want to do what's best for them—but what's "best" for them isn't always clear. Sociologist Annette Lareau surveyed and observed parents and children from **middle-class**, **working-class**, and poor backgrounds to see how their parenting styles differed. Her findings clearly showed that these groups of parents had very different ideas of what was best for their children. Lareau acknowledges that there is no best way to parent, but she argues that the differences in these parents' ideas are socially significant. As you read, consider whether kids like Alexander Williams and Harold McAllister will succeed—and be happy—in life, and how much of that has to do with how they are reared.

IN RECENT DECADES, SOCIOLOGICAL KNOWLEDGE ABOUT IN-equality in family life has increased dramatically. Yet, debate persists, especially about the transmission of class advantages to children. Kingston (2000) and others question whether disparate aspects of family life cohere in meaningful patterns. Pointing to a "thin evidentiary base" for claims of social class differences in the interior of family life, Kingston also asserts that "class distinguishes neither distinctive parenting styles or distinctive involvement of kids" in specific behaviors (p. 134).

One problem with many studies is that they are narrowly focused. Researchers look at the influence of parents' education on parent involvement in schooling *or* at children's time spent watching television *or* at time spent visiting relatives. Only a few studies examine more than one dynamic inside the home. Second, much of the empirical work is descriptive. For example, extensive research has been done on time use, including patterns of women's labor force participation, hours parents spend at work, and mothers' and fathers' contributions to childcare (Hertz and Marshall 2001; Jacobs and Gerson 1998; Menaghan 1991). Time parents spend with children also has been examined (Bianchi 2000; Bianchi and Robinson 1997; Marsiglio 1991; Presser 1989; Zick and Bryant 1996), as well as patterns of children's time use (Hofferth and Sandberg 2001b; Juster and Stafford 1985; Sandberg and Hofferth 2001). But these works have not given sufficient attention to the meaning of events or to the ways different family contexts may affect how a given task is executed (but see Daley 2001; Rubin 1976; Thorne 2001).

Third, researchers have not satisfactorily explained how these observed patterns are produced. Put differently, *conceptualizations* of the *social processes* through which families differ are underdeveloped and little is known about how family life transmits advantages to children. Few researchers have attempted to integrate what is known about behaviors and attitudes taught inside the home with the ways in which these practices may provide unequal resources for family members outside the home. A key exception is the work by Kohn and colleagues (e.g., Kohn and Schooler 1983), where the authors argue that middle-class parents value self-direction while working-class parents place a premium on "conformity to external authority." These researchers did not investigate, however, how parents go about translating these beliefs into actions.

Fourth, little is known about the degree to which children adopt and enact their parents' beliefs. Sociologists of the family have long stressed the importance of a more dynamic model of parent-child interaction (Skolnick 1991), but empirical research has been slow to emerge (but see Hess and Handel 1974). Ethnographers' efforts to document children's agency have provided vivid but highly circumscribed portraits (Shehan 1999; Waksler 1991), but most of the case studies look at only one social class or one ethnic group. Moreover, ethnographers typically do not explicitly examine how social class advantages are transmitted to children.

I draw on findings from a small, intensive data set collected using ethnographic methods. I map the connections between parents' resources and their children's daily lives. My first goal, then, is to challenge Kingston's (2000) argument that social class does not distinguish parents' behavior or children's daily lives. I seek to show empirically that social class does indeed create distinctive parenting styles. I demonstrate that parents differ by class in the ways they define their own roles in their children's lives as well as in how they perceive the nature of childhood. The middle-class parents, both white *and* black, tend to conform to a cultural logic of childrearing I call "concerted cultivation." They enroll their children in numerous age-specific organized activities that dominate family life and create enormous labor, particularly for mothers. The parents view these activities as transmitting important life skills to children. Middle-class parents also stress language use and the development of rea-soning and employ talking as their preferred form of discipline. This "cultivation" approach results in a wider range of experiences for children but also creates a frenetic pace for parents, a cult of individualism within the family, and an emphasis on chil-dren's performance.[1]

The childrearing strategies of white and black working-class and poor parents emphasize the "accomplishment of natural growth."[2] These parents believe that as long as they provide love, food, and safety, their children will grow and thrive. They do not focus on developing their children's special talents. Compared to the middle-class children, working-class and poor children participate in few organized activities and have more free time and deeper, richer ties within their extended families. Working-class and poor parents issue many more directives to their children and, in some households, place more emphasis on physical discipline than do the middle-class par-ents. These findings extend Kohn and Schooler's (1983) observation of class differ-ences in parents' values, showing that differences also exist in the *behavior* of parents *and* children.

Quantitative studies of children's activities offer valuable empirical evidence but only limited ideas about how to conceptualize the mechanisms through which social advantage is transmitted. Thus, my second goal is to offer "conceptual umbrellas" use-ful for making comparisons across race and class and for assessing the role of social structural location in shaping daily life.[3]

Last, I trace the connections between the class position of family members—including children—and the uneven outcomes of their experiences outside the home as they interact with professionals in dominant institutions. The pattern of concerted cultivation encourages an *emerging sense of entitlement* in children. All parents and children are not equally assertive, but the pattern of questioning and intervening among the white and black middle-class parents contrasts sharply with the definitions

---

[1] In a study of mothers' beliefs about childrearing, Hays (1996) found variations in how working-class and middle-class mothers sorted information, but she concluded that a pattern of "intensive mothering" was present across social classes. My study of behavior found class differences but, as I discuss below, in some instances working-class and poor parents expressed a desire to enroll their children in organized activities.

[2] Some significant differences between the study's working-class and poor families (e.g., only the poor children experienced food shortages) are not highlighted here because, on the dimensions discussed in this paper, the biggest differences were between middle-class and non-middle-class families. See Lareau (forthcoming) for a more elaborate discussion as well as Lamont (2000) for distinctions working-class families draw between themselves and the poor; see McLanahan and Sandefur (1994) regarding family structure and children's lives.

[3] Case studies of nonrandom samples, such as this one, have the limitation that findings cannot be generalized beyond the cases reported. These examples serve to illustrate conceptual points (Burawoy et al. 1991) rather than to describe representative patterns of behavior. A further limita-tion of this study is that the data were collected and analyzed over an extended period of time. (see the "Methodology" section).

of how to be helpful and effective observed among the white and black working-class and poor adults. The pattern of the accomplishment of natural growth encourages an *emerging sense of constraint.* Adults as well as children in these social classes tend to be deferential and outwardly accepting in their interactions with professionals such as doctors and educators. At the same time, however, compared to their middle-class counterparts, white and black working-class and poor family members are more distrustful of professionals. These are differences with potential long-term consequences. In an historical moment when the dominant society privileges active, informed, assertive clients of health and educational services, the strategies employed by children and parents are not equally effective across classes. In sum, differences in family life lie not only in the advantages parents obtain for their children, but also in the skills they transmit to children for negotiating their own life paths.

* * *

CONCERTED CULTIVATION AND NATURAL GROWTH

The interviews and observations suggested that crucial aspects of family life *cohered.* Within the concerted cultivation and accomplishment of natural growth approaches, three key dimensions may be distinguished: the organization of daily life, the use of language, and social connections. ("Interventions in institutions" and "consequences" are addressed later in the paper.) These dimensions do not capture all important parts of family life, but they do incorporate core aspects of childrearing (Table 1). Moreover, our field observations revealed that behaviors and activities related to these dimensions dominated the rhythms of family life. Conceptually, the organization of daily life and the use of language are crucial dimensions. Both must be present for the family to be described as engaging in one childrearing approach rather than the other. Social connections are significant but less conceptually essential.

All three aspects of childrearing were intricately woven into the families' daily routines, but rarely remarked upon. As part of everyday practice, they were invisible to parents and children. Analytically, however, they are useful means for comparing and contrasting ways in which social class differences shape the character of family life. I now examine two families in terms of these three key dimensions. I "control" for race and gender and contrast the lives of two black boys—one from an (upper) middle-class family and one from a family on public assistance. I could have focused on almost any of the other 12 children, but this pair seemed optimal, given the limited number of studies reporting on black middle-class families, as well as the aspect of my argument that suggests that race is less important than class in shaping childrearing patterns.

TABLE 1. Summary of Differences in Childrearing Approaches

Dimension Observed	Childrearing Approach	
	Concerted Cultivation	Accomplishment of Natural Growth
Key elements of each approach	Parent actively fosters and assesses child's talents, opinions, and skills	Parent cares for child and allows child to grow
Organization of daily life	Multiple child leisure activities are orchestrated by adults	Child "hangs out" particularly with kin
Language use	Reasoning/directives	Directives
	Child contestation of adult statements	Rare for child to question or challenge adults
	Extended negotiations between parents and child	General acceptance by child of directives
Social connections	Weak extended family ties	Strong extended family ties
	Child often in homogenous age groupings	Child often in heterogeneous age groupings
Interventions in institutions	Criticisms and interventions on behalf of child	Dependence on institutions
	Training of child to intervene on his or her own behalf	Sense of powerlessness and frustration
		Conflict between childrearing practices at home and at school
Consequences	Emerging sense of entitlement on the part of the child	Emerging sense of constraint on the part of the child

Developing Alexander Williams

Alexander Williams and his parents live in a predominantly black middle-class neighborhood. Their six-bedroom house is worth about $150,000.[4] Alexander is an only child. Both parents grew up in small towns in the South, and both are from large families. His father, a tall, handsome man, is a very successful trial lawyer who earns about $125,000 annually in a small firm specializing in medical malpractice cases. Two weeks each month, he works very long hours (from about 5:30 A.M. until midnight) preparing for trials. The other two weeks, his workday ends around 6:00 P.M. He rarely travels out of town. Alexander's mother, Christina, is a positive, bubbly woman with freckles and long, black, wavy hair.[5] A high-level manager in a major corporation, she has a corner office, a personal secretary, and responsibilities for other offices

---

[4] Mr. and Ms. Williams disagreed about the value of their home; the figure here averages what each reported in 1995. Housing prices in their region were lower—and continue to be lower today—than in many other parts of the country. Their property is now worth an estimated $175,000 to $200,000.

[5] Alexander's mother goes by Christina Nile at work, but Mrs. Williams at church. Some other mothers' last names also differ from their children's. Here I assign all mothers the same last names as their children.

across the nation. She tries to limit her travel, but at least once a month she takes an overnight trip.

Alexander is a charming, inquisitive boy with a winsome smile. Ms. Williams is pleased that Alexander seems interested in so many things:

> Alexander is a joy. He's a gift to me. He's very energetic, very curious, loving, caring person, that, um ... is outgoing and who, uh, really loves to be with people. And who loves to explore, and loves to read and ... just do a lot of fun things.

The private school Alexander attends[6] has an on-site after-school program. There, he participates in several activities and receives guitar lessons and photography instruction.

Organization of daily life Alexander is busy with activities during the week and on weekends (Table 2). His mother describes their Saturday morning routine. The day starts early with a private piano lesson for Alexander downtown, a 20-minute drive from the house:

> It's an 8:15 class. But for me, it was a tradeoff. I am very adamant about Saturday morning TV. I don't know what it contributes. So ... it was ... um ... either stay at home and fight on a Saturday morning [laughs] or go do something constructive ... Now Saturday mornings are pretty booked up. You know, the piano lesson, and then straight to choir for a couple of hours. So, he has a very full schedule.

Ms. Williams's vehement opposition to television is based on her view of what Alexander needs to grow and thrive. She objects to TV's passivity and feels it is her obligation to help her son cultivate his talents.

Sometimes Alexander complains that "my mother signs me up for everything!" Generally, however, he likes his activities. He says they make him feel "special," and without them life would be "boring." His sense of time is thoroughly entwined with his activities: He feels disoriented when his schedule is not full. This unease is clear in the following field-note excerpt. The family is driving home from a Back-to-School night. The next morning, Ms. Williams will leave for a work-related day trip and will not return until late at night. Alexander is grumpy because he has nothing planned for the next day. He wants to have a friend over, but his mother rebuffs him. Whining, he wonders what he will do. His mother, speaking tersely, says:

> You have piano and guitar. You'll have some free time. [Pause] I think you'll survive for one night. [Alexander does not respond but seems mad. It is quiet for the rest of the trip home.]

---

[6] I contacted the Williams family through social networks after I was unable to recruit the black middle-class families who had participated in the classroom observation and interview phase. As a result, I do not have data from classroom observations or parent-teacher conferences for Alexander.

TABLE 2. Participation in Activities Outside of School: Boys

Boy's Name/ Race/Class	Activities Organized by Adults	Informal Activities
Middle Class		
Garrett Tallinger (white)	Soccer team Traveling soccer team Baseball team Basketball team (summer) Swim team Piano Saxophone (through school)	Plays with siblings in yard Watches television Plays computer games Overnights with friends
Alexander Williams (black)	Soccer team Baseball team Community choir Church choir Sunday school Piano (Suzuki) School plays Guitar (through school)	Restricted television Plays outside occasionally with two other boys Visits friends from school
Working Class		
Billy Yanelli (white)	Baseball team	Watches television Visits relatives Rides bike Plays outside in the street Hangs out with neighborhood kids
Tyrec Taylor (black)	Football team Vacation Bible School Sunday school (off/on)	Watches television Plays outside in the street Rides bikes with neighborhood boys Visits relatives Goes to swimming pool
Poor		
Karl Greeley (white)	Goes to swimming pool Walks dogs with neighbor	Watches television Plays Nintendo Plays with siblings
Harold McAllister (black)	Bible study in neighbor's house (occasionally) Bible camp (1 week)	Visits relatives Plays ball with neighborhood kids Watches television Watches videos

Alexander's parents believe his activities provide a wide range of benefits important for his development. In discussing Alexander's piano lessons, Mr. Williams notes that as a Suzuki student,[7] Alexander is already able to read music. Speculating about more diffuse benefits of Alexander's involvement with piano, he says:

---

[7] The Suzuki method is labor intensive. Students are required to listen to music about one hour per day. Also, both child and parent(s) are expected to practice daily and to attend every lesson together.

I don't see how any kid's adolescence and adulthood could not but be enhanced by an awareness of who Beethoven was. And is that Bach or Mozart? I don't know the difference between the two! I don't know Baroque from Classical—but he does. How can that not be a benefit in later life? I'm convinced that this rich experience will make him a better person, a better citizen, a better husband, a better father—certainly a better student.

Ms. Williams sees music as building her son's "confidence" and his "poise." In interviews and casual conversation, she stresses "exposure." She believes it is her responsibility to broaden Alexander's worldview. Childhood activities provide a learning ground for important life skills:

> Sports provide great opportunities to learn how to be competitive. Learn how to accept defeat, you know. Learn how to accept winning, you know, in a gracious way. Also it gives him the opportunity to learn leadership skills and how to be a team player.... Sports really provides a lot of really great opportunities.

Alexander's schedule is constantly shifting; some activities wind down and others start up. Because the schedules of sports practices and games are issued no sooner than the start of the new season, advance planning is rarely possible. Given the sheer number of Alexander's activities, events inevitably overlap. Some activities, though short-lived, are extremely time consuming. Alexander's school play, for example, requires rehearsals three nights the week before the opening. In addition, in choosing activities, the Williamses have an added concern—the group's racial balance. Ms. Williams prefers that Alexander not be the only black child at events. Typically, one or two other black boys are involved, but the groups are predominantly white and the activities take place in predominantly white residential neighborhoods. Alexander is, however, part of his church's youth choir and Sunday School, activities in which all participants are black.

Many activities involve competition. Alex must audition for his solo performance in the school play, for example. Similarly, parents and children alike understand that participation on "A," "B," or "All-Star" sports teams signal different skill levels. Like other middle-class children in the study, Alexander seems to enjoy public performance. According to a field note, after his solo at a musical production in front of over 200 people, he appeared "contained, pleased, aware of the attention he's receiving."

Alexander's commitments do not consume *all* his free time. Still, his life is defined by a series of deadlines and schedules interwoven with a series of activities that are organized and controlled by adults rather than children. Neither he nor his parents see this as troublesome.

Language use Like other middle-class families, the Williamses often engage in conversation that promotes reasoning and negotiation. An excerpt from a field note (describing an exchange between Alexander and his mother during a car ride home after summer camp) shows the kind of pointed questions middle-class parents ask children. Ms. Williams is not just eliciting information. She is also giving Alexander the opportunity to develop and practice verbal skills, including how to summarize, clarify, and amplify information:

> As she drives, [Ms. Williams] asks Alex, "So, how was your day?"
>
> *Alex:* "Okay. I had hot dogs today, but they were burned! They were all black!"
>
> *Mom:* "Oh, great. You shouldn't have eaten any."
>
> *Alex:* "They weren't *all* black, only half were. The rest were regular."
>
> *Mom:* "Oh, okay. What was that game you were playing this morning? . . .
>
> *Alex:* "It was [called] 'Whatcha doin?'"
>
> *Mom:* "How do you play?"

Alexander explains the game elaborately—fieldworker doesn't quite follow. Mom asks Alex questions throughout his explanation, saying, "Oh, I see," when he answers. She asks him about another game she saw them play; he again explains. . . . She continues to prompt and encourage him with small giggles in the back of her throat as he elaborates.

Expressions of interest in children's activities often lead to negotiations over small, home-based matters. During the same car ride, Ms. Williams tries to adjust the dinner menu to suit Alexander:

> Alexander says, "I don't want hot dogs tonight."
>
> *Mom:* "Oh? Because you had them for lunch."
>
> Alexander nods.
>
> *Mom:* "Well, I can fix something else and save the hot dogs for tomorrow night."
>
> *Alex:* "But I don't want any pork chops either."
>
> *Mom:* "Well, Alexander, we need to eat something. Why didn't you have hamburgers today?"
>
> *Alex:* "They don't have them any more at the snack bar."
>
> Mom asks Alexander if he's ok, if he wants a snack. Alexander says he's ok. Mom asks if he's sure he doesn't want a bag of chips?

Not all middle-class parents are as attentive to their children's needs as this mother, and none are *always* interested in negotiating. But a general pattern of reasoning and accommodating is common.

Social connections Mr. and Ms. Williams consider themselves very close to their extended families. Because the Williams's aging parents live in the South, visiting requires a plane trip. Ms. Williams takes Alexander with her to see his grandparents twice a year. She speaks on the phone with her parents at least once a week and also calls her siblings several times a week. Mr. Williams talks with his mother regularly by phone (he has less contact with his stepfather). With pride, he also mentions his niece, whose Ivy League education he is helping to finance.

Interactions with cousins are not normally a part of Alexander's leisure time. (As I explain below, other middle-class children did not see cousins routinely either, even when they lived nearby.) Nor does he often play with neighborhood children. The huge homes on the Williams's street are occupied mainly by couples without children. Most of Alexander's playmates come from his classroom or his organized activities. Because most of his school events, church life, and assorted activities are organized by the age (and sometimes gender) of the participants, Alexander interacts almost exclusively with children his own age, usually boys. Adult-organized activities thus define the context of his social life.

Mr. and Ms. Williams are aware that they allocate a sizable portion of time to Alexander's activities. What they stress, however, is the time they *hold back*. They mention activities the family has chosen *not* to take on (such as traveling soccer).

Summary Overall, Alexander's parents engaged in concerted cultivation. They fostered their son's growth through involvement in music, church, athletics, and academics. They talked with him at length, seeking his opinions and encouraging his ideas. Their approach involved considerable direct expenses (e.g., the cost of lessons and equipment) and large indirect expenses (e.g., the cost of taking time off from work, driving to practices, and foregoing adult leisure activities). Although Mr. and Ms. Williams acknowledged the importance of extended family, Alexander spent relatively little time with relatives. His social interactions occurred almost exclusively with children his own age and with adults. Alexander's many activities significantly shaped the organization of daily life in the family. Both parents' leisure time was tailored to their son's commitments. Mr. and Ms. Williams felt that the strategies they cultivated with Alexander would result in his having the best possible chance at a happy and productive life. They couldn't imagine themselves *not* investing large amounts of time and energy in their son's life. But, as I explain in the next section, which focuses on a black boy from a poor family, other parents held a different view.

Supporting the Natural Growth of Harold McAllister

Harold McAllister, a large, stocky boy with a big smile, is from a poor black family. He lives with his mother and his 8-year-old sister, Alexis, in a large apartment. Two cousins often stay overnight. Harold's 16-year-old sister and 18-year-old brother usually live with their grandmother, but sometimes they stay at the McAllister's home. Ms. McAllister, a high school graduate, relies on public assistance (AFDC). Hank, Harold and Alexis's father, is a mechanic. He and Ms. McAllister have never married. He visits regularly, sometimes weekly, stopping by after work to watch television or nap. Harold (but not Alexis) sometimes travels across town by bus to spend the weekend with Hank.

The McAllister's apartment is in a public housing project near a busy street. The complex consists of rows of two- and three-story brick units. The buildings, blocky and brown, have small yards enclosed by concrete and wood fences. Large floodlights are mounted on the corners of the buildings, and wide concrete sidewalks cut through the spaces between units. The ground is bare in many places; paper wrappers and glass litter the area.

Inside the apartment, life is humorous and lively, with family members and kin sharing in the daily routines. Ms. McAllister discussed, disdainfully, mothers who are on drugs or who abuse alcohol and do not "look after" their children. Indeed, the previous year Ms. McAllister called Child Protective Services to report her twin sister, a cocaine addict, because she was neglecting her children. Ms. McAllister is actively involved in her twin's daughters' lives. Her two nephews also frequently stay with her. Overall, she sees herself as a capable mother who takes care of her children and her extended family.

Organization of daily life Much of Harold's life and the lives of his family members revolve around home. Project residents often sit outside in lawn chairs or on front stoops, drinking beer, talking, and watching children play. During summer, windows are frequently left open, allowing breezes to waft through the units and providing vantage points from which residents can survey the neighborhood. A large deciduous tree in front of the McAllister's apartment unit provides welcome shade in the summer's heat.

Harold loves sports. He is particularly fond of basketball, but he also enjoys football, and he follows televised professional sports closely. Most afternoons, he is either inside watching television or outside playing ball. He tosses a football with cousins and boys from the neighboring units and organizes pick-up basketball games. Sometimes he and his friends use a rusty, bare hoop hanging from a telephone pole in the housing project; other times, they string up an old, blue plastic crate as a makeshift hoop. One obstacle to playing sports, however, is a shortage of equipment. Balls are costly to replace, especially given the rate at which they disappear—theft of children's play equipment, including balls and bicycles, is an ongoing problem. During a field observation, Harold asks his mother if she knows where the ball is. She replies with some vehemence, "They stole the blue and yellow ball, and they stole the green ball, and they stole the other ball."

Hunting for balls is a routine part of Harold's leisure time. One June day, with the temperature and humidity in the high 80's, Harold and his cousin Tyrice (and a fieldworker) wander around the housing project for about an hour, trying to find a basketball:

> We head to the other side of the complex. On the way . . . we passed four guys sitting on the step. Their ages were 9 to 13 years. They had a radio blaring. Two were working intently on fixing a flat bike tire. The other two were dribbling a basketball.

Harold: "Yo! What's up, ya'll."

Group: "What's up, Har." "What's up?" "Yo."

They continued to work on the tire and dribble the ball. As we walked down the hill, Harold asked, "Yo, could I use your ball?"
The guy responded, looking up from the tire, "Naw, man. Ya'll might lose it."

Harold, Tyrice, and the fieldworker walk to another part of the complex, heading for a makeshift basketball court where they hope to find a game in progress:

No such luck. Harold enters an apartment directly in front of the makeshift court. The door was open. . . . Harold came back. "No ball. I guess I gotta go back."

The pace of life for Harold and his friends ebbs and flows with the children's interests and family obligations. The day of the basketball search, for example, after spending time listening to music and looking at baseball cards, the children join a water fight Tyrice instigates. It is a lively game, filled with laughter and with efforts to get the adults next door wet (against their wishes). When the game winds down, the kids ask their mother for money, receive it, and then walk to a store to buy chips and soda. They chat with another young boy and then amble back to the apartment, eating as they walk. Another afternoon, almost two weeks later, the children—Harold, two of his cousins, and two children from the neighborhood—and the fieldworker play basketball on a makeshift court in the street (using the fieldworker's ball). As Harold bounces the ball, neighborhood children of all ages wander through the space.

Thus, Harold's life is more free-flowing and more child-directed than is Alexander Williams's. The pace of any given day is not so much planned as emergent, reflecting child-based interests and activities. Parents intervene in specific areas, such as personal grooming, meals, and occasional chores, but they do not continuously direct and monitor their children's leisure activities. Moreover, the leisure activities Harold and other working-class and poor children pursue require them to develop a repertoire of skills for dealing with much older and much younger children as well as with neighbors and relatives.

Language use Life in the working-class and poor families in the study flows smoothly without extended verbal discussions. The amount of talking varies, but overall, it is considerably less than occurs in the middle-class homes.[8] Ms. McAllister jokes with the children and discusses what is on television. But she does not appear to cultivate conversation by asking the children questions or by drawing them out. Often she is brief and direct in her remarks. For instance, she coordinates the use of the

---

[8] Hart and Risley (1995) reported a similar difference in speech patterns. In their sample, by about age three, children of professionals had larger vocabularies and spoke more utterances per hour than the *parents* of similarly aged children on welfare.

apartment's only bathroom by using one-word directives. She sends the children (there are almost always at least four children home at once) to wash up by pointing to a child, saying one word, "bathroom," and handing him or her a washcloth. Wordlessly, the designated child gets up and goes to the bathroom to take a shower.

Similarly, although Ms. McAllister will listen to the children's complaints about school, she does not draw them out on these issues or seek to determine details, as Ms. Williams would. For instance, at the start of the new school year, when I ask Harold about his teacher, he tells me she is "mean" and that "she lies." Ms. McAllister, washing dishes, listens to her son, but she does not encourage Harold to support his opinion about his new teacher with more examples, nor does she mention any concerns of her own. Instead, she asks about last year's teacher, "What was the name of that man teacher?" Harold says, "Mr. Lindsey?" She says, "No, the other one." He says, "Mr. Terrene." Ms. McAllister smiles and says, "Yeah. I liked him." Unlike Alexander's mother, she seems content with a brief exchange of information.

Social connections Children, especially boys, frequently play outside. The number of potential playmates in Harold's world is vastly higher than the number in Alexander's neighborhood. When a fieldworker stops to count heads, she finds 40 children of elementary school age residing in the nearby rows of apartments. With so many children nearby, Harold could choose to play only with others his own age. In fact, though, he often hangs out with older and younger children and with his cousins (who are close to his age).

The McAllister family, like other poor and working-class families, is involved in a web of extended kin. As noted earlier, Harold's older siblings and his two male cousins often spend the night at the McAllister home. Celebrations such as birthdays involve relatives almost exclusively. Party guests are not, as in middle-class families, friends from school or from extra-curricular activities. Birthdays are celebrated enthusiastically, with cake and special food to mark the occasion; presents, however, are not offered. Similarly, Christmas at Harold's house featured a tree and special food but no presents. At these and other family events, the older children voluntarily look after the younger ones: Harold plays with his 16-month-old niece, and his cousins carry around the younger babies.

The importance of family ties—and the contingent nature of life in the McAllister's world—is clear in the response Alexis offers when asked what she would do if she were given a million dollars:

> Oh, boy! I'd buy my brother, my sister, my uncle, my aunt, my nieces and my nephews, and my grandpop, and my grandmom, and my mom, and my dad, and my friends, not my friends, but mostly my best friend—I'd buy them all clothes . . . and sneakers. And I'd buy some food, and I'd buy my mom some food, and I'd get my brothers and my sisters gifts for their birthdays.

Summary In a setting where everyone, including the children, was acutely aware of the lack of money, the McAllister family made do. Ms. McAllister rightfully saw herself as a very capable mother. She was a strong, positive influence in the lives of the children she looked after. Still, the contrast with Ms. Williams is striking. Ms. McAllister did not seem to think that Harold's opinions needed to be cultivated and developed. She, like most parents in the working-class and poor families, drew strong and clear boundaries between adults and children. Adults gave directions to children. Children were given freedom to play informally unless they were needed for chores. Extended family networks were deemed important and trustworthy.

The Intersection of Race and Class in Family Life

I expected race to powerfully shape children's daily schedules, but this was not evident (also see Conley 1999; Pattillo-McCoy 1999). This is not to say that race is unimportant. Black parents were particularly concerned with monitoring their children's lives outside the home for signs of racial problems.[9] Black middle-class fathers, especially, were likely to stress the importance of their sons understanding "what it means to be a black man in this society" (J. Hochschild 1995). Mr. Williams, in summarizing how he and his wife orient Alexander, said:

> [We try to] teach him that race unfortunately is the most important aspect of our national life. I mean people look at other people and they see a color first. But that isn't going to define who he is. He will do his best. He will succeed, despite racism. And I think he lives his life that way.

Alexander's parents were acutely aware of the potential significance of race in his life. Both were adamant, however, that race should not be used as "an excuse" for not striving to succeed. Mr. Williams put it this way:

> I discuss how race impacts on my life as an attorney, and I discuss how race will impact on his life. The one teaching that he takes away from this is that he is never to use discrimination as an excuse for not doing his best.

Thus far, few incidents of overt racism had occurred in Alexander's life, as his mother noted:

> Those situations have been far and few between. . . . I mean, I can count them on my fingers.

Still, Ms. Williams recounted with obvious pain an incident at a birthday party Alexander had attended as a preschooler. The grandparents of the birthday child

---

[9] This section focuses primarily on the concerns of black parents. Whites, of course, also benefited from race relations, notably in the scattering of poor white families in working-class neighborhoods rather than being concentrated in dense settings with other poor families (Massey and Denton 1993).

repeatedly asked, "Who is that boy?" and exclaimed, "He's so dark!" Such experiences fueled the Williams's resolve always to be "cautious":

> We've never been, uh, parents who drop off their kid anywhere. We've always gone with him. And even now, I go in and—to school in the morning—and check [in]. . . . The school environment, we've watched very closely.

Alexander's parents were not equally optimistic about the chances for racial equality in this country. Ms. Williams felt strongly that, especially while Alexander was young, his father should not voice his pessimism. Mr. Williams complained that this meant he had to "watch" what he said to Alexander about race relations. Still, both parents agreed about the need to be vigilant regarding potential racial problems in Alexander's life. Other black parents reported experiencing racial prejudice and expressed a similar commitment to vigilance.

Issues surrounding the prospect of growing up black and male in this society were threaded through Alexander's life in ways that had no equivalent among his middle-class, white male peers. Still, in fourth grade there were no signs of racial experiences having "taken hold" the way that they might as Alexander ages. In terms of the number and kind of activities he participated in, his life was very similar to that of Garrett Tallinger, his white counterpart (see Table 2). That both sets of parents were fully committed to a strategy of concentrated cultivation was apparent in the number of adult-organized activities the boys were enrolled in, the hectic pace of family life, and the stress on reasoning in parent-child negotiations. Likewise, the research assistants and I saw no striking differences in the ways in which white parents and black parents in the working-class and poor homes socialized their children.

Others (Fordham and Ogbu 1986) have found that in middle school and high school, adolescent peer groups often draw sharp racial boundaries, a pattern not evident among this study's third- and fourth-grade participants (but sometimes present among their older siblings). Following Tatum (1997:52), I attribute this to the children's relatively young ages (also see "Race in America." *The New York Times,* June 25, 2000, p. 1). In sum, in the broader society, key aspects of daily life were shaped by racial segregation and discrimination. But in terms of enrollment in organized activities, language use, and social connections, the largest differences between the families we observed were across social class, not racial groups.

DIFFERENCES IN CULTURAL PRACTICES ACROSS THE TOTAL SAMPLE

The patterns observed among the Williams and McAllister families occurred among others in the 12-family subsample and across the larger group of 88 children.

Frequently, they also echoed established patterns in the literature. These patterns highlight not only the amount of time spent on activities but also the quality of family life and the ways in which key dimensions of childrearing intertwine.

* * *

IMPACT OF CHILDREARING STRATEGIES ON INTERACTIONS WITH INSTITUTIONS

Social scientists sometimes emphasize the importance of reshaping parenting practices to improve children's chances of success. Explicitly and implicitly, the literature exhorts parents to comply with the views of professionals (Bronfenbrenner 1966; Epstein 2001; Heimer and Staffen 1998). Such calls for compliance do not, however, reconcile professionals' judgments regarding the intrinsic value of current childrearing standards with the evidence of the historical record, which shows regular shifts in such standards over time (Aries 1962; Wrigley 1989; Zelizer 1985). Nor are the stratified, and limited, possibilities for success in the broader society examined.

I now follow the families out of their homes and into encounters with representatives of dominant institutions—institutions that are directed by middle-class professionals. Again, I focus on Alexander Williams and Harold McAllister. (Institutional experiences are summarized in Table 1.) Across all social classes, parents and children interacted with teachers and school officials, healthcare professionals, and assorted government officials. Although they often addressed similar problems (e.g., learning disabilities, asthma, traffic violations), they typically did not achieve similar resolutions. The pattern of concerted cultivation fostered an *emerging sense of entitlement* in the life of Alexander Williams and other middle-class children. By contrast, the commitment to nurturing children's natural growth fostered an *emerging sense of constraint* in the life of Harold McAllister and other working-class or poor children. (These consequences of childrearing practices are summarized in Table 1.)

Both parents and children drew on the resources associated with these two childrearing approaches during their interactions with officials. Middle-class parents and children often customized these interactions; working-class and poor parents were more likely to have a "generic" relationship. When faced with problems, middle-class parents also appeared better equipped to exert influence over other adults compared with working-class and poor parents. Nor did middle-class parents or children display the intimidation or confusion we witnessed among many working-class and poor families when they faced a problem in their children's school experience.

Emerging Signs of Entitlement

Alexander Williams's mother, like many middle-class mothers, explicitly teaches her son to be an informed, assertive client in interactions with professionals. For example, as she drives Alexander to a routine doctor's appointment, she coaches him in the art of communicating effectively in healthcare settings:

> Alexander asks if he needs to get any shots today at the doctor's. Ms. Williams says he'll need to ask the doctor. . . . As we enter Park Lane, Mom says quietly to Alex: "Alexander, you should be thinking of questions you might want to ask the doctor. You can ask him anything you want. Don't be shy. You can ask anything."

> Alex thinks for a minute, then: "I have some bumps under my arms from my deodorant."
>
> *Mom:* "Really? You mean from your new deodorant?"
>
> *Alex:* "Yes."
>
> *Mom:* "Well, you should ask the doctor."

Alexander learns that he has the right to speak up (e.g., "don't be shy") and that he should prepare for an encounter with a person in a position of authority by gathering his thoughts in advance.

These class resources are subsequently *activated* in the encounter with the doctor (a jovial white man in his late thirties or early forties). The examination begins this way:

> Doctor: "Okay, as usual, I'd like to go through the routine questions with you. And if you have any questions for me, just fire away." Doctor examines Alex's chart: "Height-wise, as usual, Alexander's in the ninety-fifth percentile."

Although the physician is talking to Ms. Williams, Alexander interrupts him:

> *Alex:* "I'm in the what?"
>
> *Doctor:* "It means that you're taller than more than ninety-five out of a hundred young men when they're, uh, ten years old."
>
> *Alex:* "I'm not ten."
>
> *Doctor:* "Well, they graphed you at ten . . . they usually take the closest year to get that graph."
>
> *Alex:* "Alright."

Alexander's "Alright" reveals that he feels entitled to weigh-in with his own judgment.

A few minutes later, the exam is interrupted when the doctor is asked to provide an emergency consultation by telephone. Alexander listens to the doctor's conversation and then uses what he has overheard as the basis for a clear directive:

> Doctor: "The stitches are on the eyelids themselves, the laceration? . . . Um . . . I don't suture eyelids . . . um . . . Absolutely not! . . . Don't even touch them. That was very bad judgment on the camp's part. . . . [Hangs up.] I'm sorry about the interruption."
>
> Alex: "Stay away from my eyelids!"

Alexander's comment, which draws laughter from the adults, reflects this fourth grader's tremendous ease interacting with a physician.

Later, Ms. Williams and the doctor discuss Alexander's diet. Ms. Williams freely admits that they do not always follow nutritional guidelines. Her honesty is a form of capital because it gives the doctor accurate information on which to base a diagnosis. Feeling no need for deception positions mother and son to receive better care:

> Doctor: "Let's start with appetite. Do you get three meals a day?"
>
> Alex: "Yeah."
>
> Doctor: "And here's the important question: Do you get your fruits and vegetables too?"
>
> Alex: "Yeah."
>
> Mom, high-pitched: "Ooooo. . . ."
>
> Doctor: "I see I have a second opinion." [laughter]
>
> Alex, voice rising: "You give me bananas and all in my lunch every day. And I had cabbage for dinner last night."
>
> Doctor: "Do you get at least one or two fruits, one or two vegetables every day?"
>
> Alex: "Yeah."
>
> Doctor: "Marginally?"
>
> Mom: "Ninety-eight percent of the time he eats pretty well."
>
> Doctor: "OK, I can live with that. . . ."

Class resources are again activated when Alexander's mother reveals she "gave up" on a medication. The doctor pleasantly but clearly instructs her to continue the medication. Again, though, he receives accurate information rather than facing silent resistance or defiance, as occurred in encounters between healthcare professionals and other (primarily working-class and poor) families. The doctor acknowledges Ms. Williams's relative power: He "argues for" continuation rather than directing her to execute a medically necessary action:

> Mom: "His allergies have just been, just acted up again. One time this summer and I had to bring him in."
>
> Doctor: "I see a note here from Dr. Svennson that she put him on Vancinace and Benadryl. Did it seem to help him?"

Mom: "Just, not really. So, I used it for about a week and I just gave up."

Doctor, sitting forward in his chair: "OK, I'm actually going to argue for not giving up. If he needs it, Vancinace is a very effective drug. But it takes at least a week to start...."

Mom: "Oh. OK...."

Doctor: "I'd rather have him use that than heavy oral medications. You have to give it a few weeks...."

A similar pattern of give and take and questioning characterizes Alexander's interaction with the doctor, as the following excerpt illustrates:

Doctor: "The only thing that you really need besides my checking you, um, is to have, um, your eyes checked downstairs."

Alex: "Yes! I love that, I love that!"

Doctor laughs: "Well, now the most important question. Do you have any questions you want to ask me before I do your physical?"

Alex: "Um.... only one. I've been getting some bumps on my arms, right around here [indicates underarm]."

Doctor: "Underneath?"

Alex: "Yeah."

Doctor: "OK.... Do they hurt or itch?"

Alex: "No, they're just there."

Doctor: "OK, I'll take a look at those bumps for you. Um, what about you—um..."

Alex: "They're barely any left."

Doctor: "OK, well, I'll take a peek.... Any questions or worries on your part?" [Looking at the mother]

Mom: "No.... He seems to be coming along very nicely."[1]

Alexander's mother's last comment reflects her view of him as a project, one that is progressing "very nicely." Throughout the visit, she signals her ease and her perception of the exam as an exchange between peers (with Alexander a legitimate participant), rather than a communication from a person in authority to his subordinates. Other middle-class parents seemed similarly comfortable. * * * Middle-class parents and children were also very assertive in situations at the public elementary school most of the middle-class children in the study attended. There were numerous conflicts during the year over matters small and large. For example, parents complained to one

---

[1] Not all professionals accommodated children's participation. Regardless of these adults' overt attitudes, though, we routinely observed that middle-class mothers monitor and intervene in their children's interactions with professionals.

another and to the teachers about the amount of homework the children were assigned. A black middle-class mother whose daughters had not tested into the school's gifted program negotiated with officials to have the girls' (higher) results from a private testing company accepted instead. The parents of a fourth-grade boy drew the school superintendent into a battle over religious lyrics in a song scheduled to be sung as part of the holiday program. The superintendent consulted the district lawyer and ultimately "counseled" the principal to be more sensitive, and the song was dropped.

Children, too, asserted themselves at school. Examples include requesting that the classroom's blinds be lowered so the sun wasn't in their eyes, badgering the teacher for permission to retake a math test for a higher grade, and demanding to know why no cupcake had been saved when an absence prevented attendance at a classroom party. In these encounters, children were not simply complying with adults' requests or asking for a repeat of an earlier experience. They were displaying an emerging sense of entitlement by urging adults to permit a customized accommodation of institutional processes to suit their preferences.

Of course, some children (and parents) were more forceful than others in their dealings with teachers, and some were more successful than others. * * * The interactions the research assistants and I observed between professionals and working-class and poor parents frequently seemed cautious and constrained. This unease is evident, for example, during a physical Harold McAllister has before going to Bible camp. Harold's mother, normally boisterous and talkative at home, is quiet. Unlike Ms. Williams, she seems wary of supplying the doctor with accurate information:

Doctor:	"Does he eat something each day—either fish, meat, or egg?"
Mom, response is low and muffled:	"Yes."
Doctor, attempting to make eye contact but mom stares intently at paper:	"A yellow vegetable?"
Mom, still no eye contact, looking at the floor:	"Yeah."
Doctor:	"A green vegetable?" Mom, looking at the doctor: "Not all the time." [Fieldworker has not seen any of the children eat a green or yellow vegetable since visits began.]
Doctor:	"No. Fruit or juice?"
Mom, low voice, little or no eye contact, looks at the doctor's scribbles on the paper he is filling out:	"Ummh humn."
Doctor:	"Does he drink milk everyday?"
Mom, abruptly, in considerably louder voice:	"Yeah."

> *Doctor:* "Cereal, bread, rice, potato, anything like that?"
>
> *Mom,* shakes her head: "Yes, definitely." [Looks at doctor.]

Ms. McAllister's knowledge of developmental events in Harold's life is uneven. She is not sure when he learned to walk and cannot recall the name of his previous doctor. And when the doctor asks, "When was the last time he had a tetanus shot?" she counters, gruffly, "What's a tetanus shot?"

Unlike Ms. Williams, who urged Alexander to share information with the doctor, Ms. McAllister squelches eight-year-old Alexis's overtures:

> *Doctor:* "Any birth mark?"
>
> *Mom* looks at doctor, shakes her head no.
>
> *Alexis,* raising her left arm, says excitedly: "I have a birth mark under my arm!"
>
> *Mom,* raising her voice and looking stern: "Will you cool out a minute?"
>
> *Mom,* again answering the doctor's question: "No."

Despite Ms. McAllister's tension and the marked change in her everyday demeanor, Harold's whole exam is not uncomfortable. There are moments of laughter. Moreover, Harold's mother is not consistently shy or passive. Before the visit begins, the doctor comes into the waiting room and calls Harold's and Alexis's names. In response, the McAllisters (and the fieldworker) stand. Ms. McAllister then beckons for her nephew Tyrice (who is about Harold's age) to come along *before* she clears this with the doctor. Later, she sends Tyrice down the hall to observe Harold being weighed; she relies on her nephew's report rather than asking for this information from the healthcare professionals.

Still, neither Harold nor his mother seemed as comfortable as Alexander had been. Alexander was used to extensive conversation at home; with the doctor, he was at ease initiating questions. Harold, who was used to responding to directives at home, primarily answered questions from the doctor, rather than posing his own. Alexander, encouraged by his mother, was assertive and confident with the doctor. Harold was reserved. Absorbing his mother's apparent need to conceal the truth about the range of foods he ate, he appeared cautious, displaying an emerging sense of constraint.

We observed a similar pattern in school interactions. Overall, the working-class and poor adults had much more distance or separation from the school than their middle-class counterparts. Ms. McAllister, for example, could be quite assertive in some settings (e.g., at the start of family observations, she visited the local drug dealer, warning him not to "mess with" the black male fieldworker).[2] But throughout the

---

[2] Ms. McAllister told me about this visit; we did not observe it. It is striking that she perceived only the black male fieldworker as being at risk.

fourth-grade parent-teacher conference, she kept her winter jacket zipped up, sat hunched over in her chair, and spoke in barely audible tones. She was stunned when the teacher said that Harold did not do homework. Sounding dumbfounded, she said, "He does it at home." The teacher denied it and continued talking. Ms. McAllister made no further comments and did not probe for more information, except about a letter the teacher said he had mailed home and that she had not received. The conference ended, having yielded Ms. McAllister few insights into Harold's educational experience.[3]

Other working-class and poor parents also appeared baffled, intimidated, and subdued in parent-teacher conferences.

* * *

In classroom observations, working-class and poor children could be quite lively and energetic, but we did not observe them try to customize their environments. They tended to react to adults' offers or, at times, to plead with educators to repeat previous experiences, such as reading a particular story, watching a movie, or going to the computer room. Compared to middle-class classroom interactions, the boundaries between adults and children seemed firmer and clearer. Although the children often resisted and tested school rules, they did not seem to be seeking to get educators to accommodate their own *individual* preferences.

Overall, then, the behavior of working-class and poor parents cannot be explained as a manifestation of their temperaments or of overall passivity; parents were quite energetic in intervening in their children's lives in other spheres. Rather, working-class and poor parents generally appeared to depend on the school (Lareau 2000), even as they were dubious of the trustworthiness of the professionals. This suspicion of professionals in dominant institutions is, at least in some instances, a reasonable response.[4] The unequal level of trust, as well as differences in the amount and quality of information divulged, can yield unequal *profits* during an historical moment when professionals applaud assertiveness and reject passivity as an inappropriate parenting strategy (Epstein 2001). Middle-class children and parents often (but not always) accrued advantages or profits from their efforts. Alexander Williams succeeded in having the doctor take his medical concerns seriously. Ms. Marshall's children ended up in the gifted program, even though they did not technically qualify. Middle-class children expect institutions to be responsive to *them* and to accommodate their individual needs. By contrast, [working class and poor children] are not learning how to

---

[3] Middle-class parents sometimes appeared slightly anxious during parent-teacher conferences, but overall, they spoke more and asked educators more questions than did working-class and poor parents.

[4] The higher levels of institutional reports of child neglect, child abuse, and other family difficulties among poor families may reflect this group's greater vulnerability to institutional intervention (e.g., see L. Gordon 1989).

make bureaucratic institutions work to their advantage. Instead, they are being given lessons in frustration and powerlessness.

WHY DOES SOCIAL CLASS MATTER?

Parents' economic resources helped create the observed class differences in child-rearing practices. Enrollment fees that middle-class parents dismissed as "negligible" were formidable expenses for less affluent families. Parents also paid for clothing, equipment, hotel stays, fast food meals, summer camps, and fundraisers. In 1994, the Tallingers estimated the cost of Garrett's activities at $4,000 annually, and that figure was not unusually high.[5] Moreover, families needed reliable private transportation and flexible work schedules to get children to and from events. These resources were disproportionately concentrated in middle-class families.

Differences in educational resources also are important. Middle-class parents' superior levels of education gave them larger vocabularies that facilitated concerted cultivation, particularly in institutional interventions. Poor and working-class parents were not familiar with key terms professionals used, such as "tetanus shot." Furthermore, middle-class parents' educational backgrounds gave them confidence when criticizing educational professionals and intervening in school matters. Working-class and poor parents viewed educators as their social superiors.

Kohn and Schooler (1983) showed that parents' occupations, especially the complexity of their work, influence their childrearing beliefs. We found that parents' work mattered, but also saw signs that the experience of adulthood itself influenced conceptions of childhood. Middle-class parents often were preoccupied with the pleasures and challenges of their work lives.[6] They tended to view childhood as a dual opportunity: a chance for play, and for developing talents and skills of value later in life. * * * Ms. Williams mentioned the value of Alexander learning to work with others by playing on a sports team. Middle-class parents, aware of the "declining fortunes" of the middle class, worried about their own economic futures and those of their children (Newman 1993). This uncertainty increased their commitment to helping their children develop broad skills to enhance their future possibilities.

Working-class and poor parents' conceptions of adulthood and childhood also appeared to be closely connected to their lived experiences. For the working class, it was the deadening quality of work and the press of economic shortages that defined

---

[5] In 2002, a single sport could cost as much as $5,000 annually. Yearly league fees for ice hockey run to $2,700; equipment costs are high as well (Halbfinger 2002).

[6] Middle-class adults do not live problem-free lives, but compared with the working class and poor, they have more varied occupational experiences and greater access to jobs with higher economic returns.

their experience of adulthood and influenced their vision of childhood. It was dependence on public assistance and severe economic shortages that most shaped poor parents' views. Families in both classes had many worries about basic issues: food shortages, limited access to healthcare, physical safety, unreliable transportation, insufficient clothing. Thinking back over their childhoods, these parents remembered hardship but also recalled times without the anxieties they now faced. Many appeared to want their own youngsters to concentrate on being happy and relaxed, keeping the burdens of life at bay until they were older.

Thus, childrearing strategies are influenced by more than parents' education. It is the interweaving of life experiences and resources, including parents' economic resources, occupational conditions, and educational backgrounds, that appears to be most important in leading middle-class parents to engage in concerted cultivation and working-class and poor parents to engage in the accomplishment of natural growth. Still, the structural location of families did not fully determine their childrearing practices. The agency of actors and the indeterminacy of social life are inevitable.

In addition to economic and social resources, are there other significant factors? If the poor and working-class families' resources were transformed overnight so that they equaled those of the middle-class families, would their cultural logic of childrearing shift as well? Or are there cultural attitudes and beliefs that are substantially independent of economic and social resources that are influencing parents' practices here? The size and scope of this study preclude a definitive answer. Some poor and working-class parents embraced principles of concerted cultivation: They wished (but could not afford) to enroll their children in organized activities (e.g., piano lessons, voice lessons), they believed listening to children was important, and they were committed to being involved in their children's schooling. Still, even when parents across all of the classes seemed committed to similar principles, their motivations differed. For example, many working-class and poor parents who wanted more activities for their children were seeking a safe haven for them. Their goal was to provide protection from harm rather than to cultivate the child's talents per se.

Some parents explicitly criticized children's schedules that involved many activities. During the parent interviews, we described the real-life activities of two children (using data from the 12 families we were observing). One schedule resembled Alexander Williams's: restricted television, required reading, and many organized activities, including piano lessons (for analytical purposes, we said that, unlike Alexander, this child disliked his piano lessons but was not allowed to quit). Summing up the attitude of the working-class and poor parents who rejected this kind of schedule,[7] one white, poor mother complained:

---

[7] Many middle-class parents remarked that forcing a child to take piano lessons was wrong. Nevertheless, they continued to stress the importance of "exposure."

I think he wants more. I think he doesn't enjoy doing what he's doing half of the time (light laughter). I think his parents are too strict. And he's not a child.

Even parents who believed this more regimented approach would pay off "job-wise" when the child was an adult still expressed serious reservations: "I think he is a sad kid," or, "He must be dead-dog tired."

Thus, working-class and poor parents varied in their beliefs. Some longed for a schedule of organized activities for their children and others did not; some believed in reasoning with children and playing an active role in schooling and others did not. Fully untangling the effects of material and cultural resources on parents and children's choices is a challenge for future research.[8]

DISCUSSION

The evidence shows that class position influences critical aspects of family life: time use, language use, and kin ties. Not all aspects of family life are affected by social class, and there is variability within class. Still, parents do transmit advantages to their children in patterns that are sufficiently consistent and identifiable to be described as a "cultural logic" of childrearing. The white and black middle-class parents engaged in practices I have termed "concerted cultivation"—they made a deliberate and sustained effort to stimulate children's development and to cultivate their cognitive and social skills. The working-class and poor parents viewed children's development as spontaneously unfolding, as long as they were provided with comfort, food, shelter, and other basic support. This commitment, too, required ongoing effort; sustaining children's natural growth despite formidable life challenges is properly viewed as an accomplishment.

In daily life, the patterns associated with each of these approaches were interwoven and mutually reinforcing. Nine-year-old middle-class children already had

---

[8] Similarly, whether concerted cultivation and the accomplishment of natural growth are new historical developments rather than modifications of earlier forms of childrearing cannot be determined from the study's findings. The "institutionalization of children's leisure" seems to be increasing (Corsaro 1997). Hays (1996) argues that families increasingly are "invaded" by the "logic of impersonal, competitive, contractual, commodified, efficient, profit-maximizing, self-interested relations" (p. 11). In addition to evidence of a new increase in children's organized activities (Sandberg and Hofferth 2001), none of the middle-class parents in the study reported having childhood schedules comparable to their children's. Change over time in parents' intervention in education and in the amount of reasoning in middle-class families also are difficult to determine accurately. Kohn and Schooler's (1983) study suggests little change with regard to reasoning, but other commentators insist there has been a rise in the amount of negotiating between parents and children (Chidekel 2002; Kropp 2001). Such debates can not be resolved without additional careful historical research.

developed a clear sense of their own talents and skills, and they differentiated themselves from siblings and friends. They were also learning to think of themselves as special and worthy of having adults devote time and energy to promoting them and their leisure activities. In the process, the boundaries between adults and children sometimes blurred; adults' leisure preferences became subordinate to their children's. The strong emphasis on reasoning in middle-class families had similar, diffuse effects. Children used their formidable reasoning skills to persuade adults to acquiesce to their wishes. The idea that children's desires should be taken seriously was routinely realized in the middle-class families we interviewed and observed. In many subtle ways, children were taught that they were entitled. Finally, the commitment to cultivating children resulted in family schedules so crowded with activities there was little time left for visiting relatives. Quantitative studies of time use have shed light on important issues, but they do not capture the interactive nature of routine, everyday activities and the varying ways they affect the texture of family life.[9]

In working-class and poor families, parents established limits; within those limits, children were free to fashion their own pastimes. Children's wishes did not guide adults' actions as frequently or as decisively as they did in middle-class homes. Children were viewed as subordinate to adults. Parents tended to issue directives rather than to negotiate. Frequent interactions with relatives rather than acquaintances or strangers created a thicker divide between families and the outside world. Implicitly and explicitly, parents taught their children to keep their distance from people in positions of authority, to be distrustful of institutions, and, at times, to resist officials' authority. Children seemed to absorb the adults' feelings of powerlessness in their institutional relationships. As with the middle class, there were important variations among working-class and poor families, and some critical aspects of family life, such as the use of humor, were immune to social class.

The role of race in children's daily lives was less powerful than I had expected. The middle-class black children's parents were alert to the potential effects of institutional discrimination on their children. Middle-class black parents also took steps to help their children develop a positive racial identity. Still, in terms of how children spend their time, the way parents use language and discipline in the home, the nature of the families' social connections, and the strategies used for intervening in institutions, white and black middle-class parents engaged in very similar, often identical, practices with their children. A similar pattern was observed in white and black working-class homes as well as in white and black poor families. Thus my data indicate that on the childrearing dynamics studied here, compared with social class, race

---

[9] The time-use differences we observed were part of the taken-for-granted aspects of daily life; they were generally unnoticed by family members. For example, the working-class Yanellis considered themselves "really busy" if they had one baseball game on Saturday and an extended family gathering on Sunday. The Tallingers and other middle-class families would have considered this a slow weekend.

was less important in children's daily lives.[1] As they enter the racially segregated words of dating, marriage, and housing markets, and as they encounter more racism in their interpersonal contact with whites (Waters 1999), the relative importance of race in the children's daily lives is likely to increase.

Differences in family dynamics and the logic of childrearing across social classes have long-term consequences. As family members moved out of the home and interacted with representatives of formal institutions, middle-class parents and children were able to negotiate more valuable outcomes than their working-class and poor counterparts. In interactions with agents of dominant institutions, working-class and poor children were learning lessons in constraint while middle-class children were developing a sense of entitlement.

It is a mistake to see either concerted cultivation or the accomplishment of natural growth as an intrinsically desirable approach. As has been amply documented, conceptions of childhood have changed dramatically over time (Wrigley 1989). Drawbacks to middle-class childrearing, including the exhaustion associated with intensive mothering and frenetic family schedules and a sapping of children's naivete that leaves them feeling too sophisticated for simple games and toys (Hays 1996), remain insufficiently highlighted.

Another drawback is that middle-class children are less likely to learn how to fill "empty time" with their own creative play, leading to a dependence on their parents to solve experiences of boredom. Sociologists need to more clearly differentiate between standards that are intrinsically desirable and standards that facilitate success in dominant institutions. A more critical, and historically sensitive, vision is needed (Donzelot 1979). Here Bourdieu's work (1976, 1984, 1986, 1989) is valuable.

Finally, there are methodological issues to consider. Quantitative research has delineated population-wide patterns; ethnographies offer rich descriptive detail but typically focus on a single, small group. Neither approach can provide holistic, but empirically grounded, assessments of daily life. Multi-sited, multi-person research using ethnographic methods also pose formidable methodological challenges (Lareau 2002). Still, families have proven themselves open to being studied in an intimate fashion. Creating penetrating portraits of daily life that will enrich our theoretical models is an important challenge for the future.

REFERENCES

Aries, Philippe. 1962. *Centuries of Childhood: A Social History of the Family.* Translated by R. Baldick. London, England: Cape.

---

[1] These findings are compatible with others showing children as aware of race at relatively early ages (Van Ausdale and Feagin 1996). At the two sites, girls often played in racially segregated groups during recess; boys tended to play in racially integrated groups.

Bianchi, Suzanne M. 2000. "Maternal Employment and Time with Children: Dramatic Change or Surprising Continuity." *Demography* 37:401–14.

Bianchi, Suzanne M. and John Robinson. 1997. "What Did You Do Today? Children's Use of Time, Family Composition, and Acquisition of Social Capital." *Journal of Marriage and the Family* 59:332–44.

Bourdieu, Pierre. 1976. "Marriage Strategies as Strategies of Social Reproduction." Pp. 117–44 in *Family and Society*, edited by R. Forster and O. Ranum. Baltimore, MD: Johns Hopkins University Press.

———. 1984. *Distinction: A Social Critique of the Judgment of Taste.* Cambridge, MA: Harvard University Press.

———. 1986. "The Forms of Capital." Pp. 241–58 in *Handbook of Theory and Research for the Sociology of Education*, edited by J. C. Richardson. New York: Greenwood.

———. 1989. *The State Nobility: Elite Schools in the Field of Power.* Stanford. CA: Stanford University Press.

Bronfenbrenner, Urie. 1966. "Socialization and Social Class through Time and Space." Pp. 362–77 in *Class, Status and Power*, edited by R. Bendix and S. M. Lipset. New York: Free Press.

Burawoy, Michael, Alice Burton, Ann Arnett Ferguson, and Kathryn J. Fox, eds. 1991. *Ethnography Unbound: Power and Resistance in the Modern Metropolis.* Berkeley, CA: University of California Press.

Chidekel, Dana. 2002. *Parents in Charge.* New York: Simon and Schuster.

Conley, Dalton. 1999. *Being Black, Living in the Red: Race, Wealth, and Social Policy in America.* Berkeley, CA: University of California Press.

Corsaro, William A. 1997. *The Sociology of Childhood.* Thousand Oaks, CA: Pine Forge.

Daley, Kerry J. 2001. "Deconstructing Family Time: From Ideology to Lived Experience." *Journal of Marriage and the Family* 63:238–94.

Donzelot, Jacques. 1979. *The Policing of Families.* Translated by R. Hurley. New York: Pantheon.

Epstein, Joyce. 2001. *Schools, Family, and Community Partnerships.* Boulder, CO: Westview.

Fordham, Signithia and John U. Ogbu. 1986. "Black Students' School Success: Coping with the 'Burden of Acting White.'" *The Urban Review* 18:176–206.

Gordon, Linda. 1989. *Heroes of Their Own Lives: The Politics and History of Family Violence.* New York: Penguin.

Halbfinger, David M. 2002. "A Hockey Parent's Life: Time, Money, and Yes, Frustration." *New York Times*, January 12, p. 29.

Hart, Betty and Todd Risley. 1995. *Meaningful Differences in the Everyday Experience of Young American Children.* Baltimore, MD: Paul Brooks.

Hays, Sharon. 1996. *The Cultural Contradictions of Motherhood.* New Haven, CT: Yale University Press.

Heimer, Carol A. and Lisa Staffen. 1998. *For the Sake of the Children: The Social Organization of Responsibility in the Hospital and at Home.* Chicago, IL: University of Chicago Press.

Hertz, Rosanna and Nancy L. Marshall, eds. 2001. *Working Families: The Transformation of the American Home.* Berkeley, CA: University of California Press.

Hess, Robert and Gerald Handel. 1974. *Family Worlds: A Psychosocial Approach to Family Life.* Chicago, IL: University of Chicago Press.

Hochschild, Jennifer L. 1995. *Facing Up to The American Dream.* Princeton, NJ: Princeton University Press.

Hofferth, Sandra and John Sandberg. 2001b. "How American Children Spend Their Time." *Journal of Marriage and the Family* 63:295–308.

Jacobs, Jerry and Kathleen Gerson. 1998. "Who Are the Overworked Americans?" *Review of Social Economy* 56:442–59.

Juster, F. Thomas and Frank P. Stafford, eds. 1985. *Time, Goods, and Well-Being.* Ann Arbor, MI: Survey Research Center, Institute for Social Research.

Kingston, Paul. 2000. *The Classless Society.* Stanford, CA: Stanford University Press.

Kohn, Melvin and Carmi Schooler, eds. 1983. *Work and Personality: An Inquiry into the Impact of Social Stratification.* Norwood, NJ: Ablex.

Kropp, Paul. 2001. *I'll Be the Parent, You Be the Child.* New York: Fisher Books.

Lamont, Michele. 2000. *The Dignity of Working Men: Morality and the Boundaries of Race, Class, and Immigration.* Cambridge, MA: Harvard University Press.

Lareau, Annette. Forthcoming. *Unequal Childhood: Class, Race, and Family Life.* Berkeley, CA: University of California Press.

———. 2002. "Doing Multi-Person, Multi-Site 'Ethnographic' Work: A Reflective, Critical Essay." Department of Sociology, Temple University, Philadelphia, PA. Unpublished manuscript.

———. 2000. *Home Advantage: Social Class and Parental Intervention in Elementary Education.* 2d ed. Lanham, MD: Rowman and Littlefield.

Marsiglio, William. 1991. "Paternal Engagement Activities with Minor Children." *Journal of Marriage and the Family* 53:973–86.

Massey, Douglas and Nancy Denton. 1993. *American Apartheid.* Cambridge, MA: Harvard University Press.

McLanahan, Sara and Gary Sandefur. 1994. *Growing Up with a Single Parent: What Hurts, What Helps.* Cambridge, MA: Harvard University Press.

Menaghan, Elizabeth G. 1991. "Work Experiences and Family Interaction Processes: The Long Reach of the Job?" *Annual Review of Sociology* 17:419–44.

Newman, Kathleen. 1993. *Declining Fortunes: The Withering of the American Dream.* New York: Basic Books.

Pattillo-McCoy, Mary 1999. *Black Picket Fences: Privilege and Peril among the Black Middle-Class.* Chicago, IL: University of Chicago Press.

Presser, Harriet B. 1989. "Can We Make Time for Children? The Economy, Work Schedules, and Child Care." *Demography* 26:523–43.

Rubin, Lillian 1976. *Worlds of Pain: Life in a Working-Class Family.* New York: Basic Books.

Sandberg, John F. and Sandra L. Hofferth. 2001. "Changes in Children's Time with Parents, U.S., 1981–1997." *Demography* 38:423–36.

Shehan, Constance L., ed. 1999. *Through the Eyes of the Child: Re-Visioning Children as Active Agents of Family Life.* New York: JAI Press.

Skolnick, Arlene. 1991. *Embattled Paradise: The American Family in an Age of Uncertainty.* New York: Basic Books.

Tatum, Beverly Daniel. 1997. *Why Are All the Black Kids Sitting Together in the Cafeteria? And Other Conversations about Race.* New York: Basic Books.

Thorne, Barrie. 2001. "Growing Up in Oakland: Orbits of Class, 'Race,' and Culture." Paper presented at the annual meeting of the American Sociological Association, August 19, Anaheim, CA.

Van Ausdale, Debra and Joe R. Feagin. 1996. "Using Racial and Ethnic Concepts: The Critical Case of Very Young Children." *American Sociological Review* 61:779–93.

Waksler, Frances. 1991. *Studying the Social Worlds of Children*. Bristol, England: Falmer.

Waters, Mary. 1999. *Black Identities: West Indian Immigrant Dreams and American Realities*. New York: Russell Sage Foundation.

Wrigley, Julia. 1989. "Do Young Children Need Intellectual Stimulation? Experts' Advice to Parents, 1900–1985." *History of Education* 29:41–75.

Zelizer, Vivianna. 1985. *Pricing the Priceless Child: The Changing Social Value of Children*. New York: Basic Books.

Zick, Cathleen D. and W. Keith Bryant. 1996. "A New Look at Parents' Time Spent in Child Care: Primary and Secondary Time Use." *Social Science Research* 25:260–80.

ACKNOWLEDGMENTS

An early version of this article was issued as a working paper by the Center for Working Families, University of California, Berkeley. I benefited from audience comments on earlier drafts presented at the American Sociological Association annual meeting in 2000, the University of California (Berkeley, Davis, and San Diego), University of Chicago, University of Pennsylvania, and Temple University. Patricia Berhau, Anita Garey, Karen Hanson, Erin McNamara Horvat, Sam Kaplan, Michele Lamont, Karen Shirley, Barrie Thorne, Elliot Weininger, and Julia Wrigley made helpful suggestions, as did the *ASR* reviewers. For funding, I thank the Spencer Foundation, Sloan Foundation, ASA/NSF Grants for the Discipline, Temple Grant-in-Aid, and Southern Illinois University. I am indebted to the project's research assistants, particularly Wendi Starr Brown, Gillian Johns, Caitlin Howley-Rowe, Greg Seaton, and Mary Woods, all of whose field notes appear in the article. I thank Nikki Johnson who assisted in production of the manuscript, and M. Katherine Mooney for editorial assistance. Errors are my responsibility.

STUDY QUESTIONS

1. According to Lareau, which is more important in determining parenting styles: **race** or **class**?

2. Harold and Alexander are being reared differently; what are some possible pros and cons of these two parenting methods?

3. Name three differences between the "concerted cultivation" and "natural growth" models. Which model most resembles your own childhood and why?

4. Divide your class or discussion group into two sections: one group should work on concerted cultivation, while the other works on the natural growth model. Each group should list the advantages and disadvantages of each style, then come back together as a full group to debate which model best prepares a child for adulthood.

JONATHAN KOZOL

The Savage Inequalities of Public Education in New York

Some U.S. students attend school in dilapidated buildings, read tattered, out-of-date textbooks, and have very few opportunities for success. At the same time, other students attend school on beautiful campuses with state-of-the-art resources and limitless opportunities. Students in the United States have very different experiences in their K–12 **education** based on where they live. Students in affluent school districts have far more resources than do their less affluent counterparts. In this essay the author explores the "savage inequalities" in public education.

* * *

IN ORDER TO FIND PUBLIC SCHOOL 261 IN DISTRICT 10, A VISITOR IS told to look for a mortician's office. The funeral home, which faces Jerome Avenue in the North Bronx, is easy to identify by its green awning. The school is next door, in a former roller-skating rink. No sign identifies the building as a school. A metal awning frame without an awning supports a flagpole, but there is no flag.

In the street in front of the school there is an elevated public transit line. Heavy traffic fills the street. The existence of the school is virtually concealed within this crowded city block.

In a vestibule between the outer and inner glass doors of the school there is a sign with these words: "All children are capable of learning."

Beyond the inner doors a guard is seated. The lobby is long and narrow. The ceiling is low. There are no windows. All the teachers that I see at first are middle-aged white women. The principal, who is also a white woman, tells me that the school's "capacity" is 900 but that there are 1,300 children here. The size of classes for fifth and sixth grade children in New York, she says, is "capped" at 32, but she says that class size in the school goes "up to 34." (I later see classes, however, as large as 37.) Classes for younger children, she goes on, are "capped at 25," but a school can go above this limit if it puts an extra adult in the room. Lack of space, she says, prevents the school from operating a pre-kindergarten program.

I ask the principal where her children go to school. They are enrolled in private school, she says.

"Lunchtime is a challenge for us," she explains. "Limited space obliges us to do it in three shifts, 450 children at a time."

Textbooks are scarce and children have to share their social studies books. The principal says there is one full-time pupil counselor and another who is here two days a week: a ratio of 930 children to one counselor. The carpets are patched and sometimes taped together to conceal an open space. "I could use some new rugs," she observes.

To make up for the building's lack of windows and the crowded feeling that results, the staff puts plants and fish tanks in the corridors. Some of the plants are flourishing. Two boys, released from class, are in a corridor beside a tank, their noses pressed against the glass. A school of pinkish fish inside the tank are darting back and forth. Farther down the corridor a small Hispanic girl is watering the plants.

Two first grade classes share a single room without a window, divided only by a blackboard. Four kindergartens and a sixth grade class of Spanish-speaking children have been packed into a single room in which, again, there is no window. A second grade bilingual class of 37 children has its own room but again there is no window.

By eleven o'clock, the lunchroom is already packed with appetite and life. The kids line up to get their meals, then eat them in ten minutes. After that, with no place they can go to play, they sit and wait until it's time to line up and go back to class.

On the second floor I visit four classes taking place within another undivided space. The room has a low ceiling. File cabinets and movable blackboards give a small degree of isolation to each class. Again, there are no windows.

The library is a tiny, windowless and claustrophobic room. I count approximately 700 books. Seeing no reference books, I ask a teacher if encyclopedias and other reference books are kept in classrooms.

"We don't have encyclopedias in classrooms," she replies. "That is for the suburbs."

The school, I am told, has 26 computers for its 1,300 children. There is one small gym and children get one period, and sometimes two, each week. Recess, however, is not possible because there is no playground. "Head Start," the principal says, "scarcely exists in District 10. We have no space."

The school, I am told, is 90 percent black and Hispanic; the other 10 percent are Asian, white or Middle Eastern.

In a sixth grade social studies class the walls are bare of words or decorations. There seems to be no ventilation system, or, if one exists, it isn't working.

The class discusses the Nile River and the Fertile Crescent.

The teacher, in a droning voice: "How is it useful that these civilizations developed close to rivers?"

A child, in a good loud voice: "What kind of question is that?"

In my notes I find these words: "An uncomfortable feeling—being in a building with no windows. There are metal ducts across the room. Do they give air? I feel asphyxiated...."

On the top floor of the school, a sixth grade of 30 children shares a room with 29 bilingual second graders. Because of the high class size there is an assistant with each teacher. This means that 59 children and four grown-ups—63 in all—must share a room that, in a suburban school, would hold no more than 20 children and one teacher. There are, at least, some outside windows in this room—it is the only room with windows in the school—and the room has a high ceiling. It is a relief to see some daylight.

I return to see the kindergarten classes on the ground floor and feel stifled once again by lack of air and the low ceiling. Nearly 120 children and adults are doing what they can to make the best of things: 80 children in four kindergarten classes, 30 children in the sixth grade class, and about eight grown-ups who are aides and teachers. The kindergarten children sitting on the worn rug, which is patched with tape, look up at me and turn their heads to follow me as I walk past them.

As I leave the school, a sixth grade teacher stops to talk. I ask her, "Is there air conditioning in warmer weather?"

Teachers, while inside the building, are reluctant to give answers to this kind of question. Outside, on the sidewalk, she is less constrained: "I had an awful room last year. In the winter it was 56 degrees. In the summer it was up to 90. It was sweltering."

I ask her, "Do the children ever comment on the building?"

"They don't say," she answers, "but they know."

I ask her if they see it as a racial message.

"All these children see TV," she says. "They know what suburban schools are like. Then they look around them at their school. This was a roller-rink, you know.... They don't comment on it but you see it in their eyes. They understand."

* * *

Two months later, on a day in May, I visit an elementary school in Riverdale. The dogwoods and magnolias on the lawn in front of P.S. 24 are in full blossom on the day I visit. There is a well-tended park across the street, another larger park three blocks away. To the left of the school is a playground for small children, with an innovative jungle gym, a slide and several climbing toys. Behind the school there are two playing fields for older kids. The grass around the school is neatly trimmed.

The neighborhood around the school, by no means the richest part of Riverdale, is nonetheless expensive and quite beautiful. Residences in the area—some of which are large, free-standing houses, others condominiums in solid red-brick buildings—sell for prices in the region of $400,000; but some of the larger Tudor houses on the winding and tree-shaded streets close to the school can cost up to $1 million. The excellence of P.S. 24, according to the principal, adds to the value of these homes. Advertisements in the *New York Times* will frequently inform prospective buyers that a house is "in the neighborhood of P.S. 24."

The school serves 825 children in the kindergarten through sixth grade. This is approximately half the student population crowded into P.S. 79, where 1,550 children fill a space intended for 1,000, and a great deal smaller than the 1,300 children packed into the former skating rink; but the principal of P.S. 24, a capable and energetic man named David Rothstein, still regards it as excessive for an elementary school.

The school is integrated in the strict sense that the middle- and upper-middle-class white children here do occupy a building that contains some Asian and Hispanic and black children; but there is little integration in the classrooms since the vast majority of the Hispanic and black children are assigned to "special" classes on the basis of evaluations that have classified them "EMR"—"educable mentally retarded"—or else, in the worst of cases, "TMR"—"trainable mentally retarded."

I ask the principal if any of his students qualify for free-lunch programs. "About 130 do," he says. "Perhaps another 35 receive their lunches at reduced price. Most of these kids are in the special classes. They do not come from this neighborhood."

The very few nonwhite children that one sees in mainstream classes tend to be Japanese or else of other Asian origins. Riverdale, I learn, has been the residence of choice for many years to members of the diplomatic corps.

The school therefore contains effectively two separate schools: one of about 130 children, most of whom are poor, Hispanic, black, assigned to one of the 12 special classes; the other of some 700 mainstream students, almost all of whom are white or Asian.

There is a third track also—this one for the students who are labeled "talented" or "gifted." This is termed a "pullout" program since the children who are so identified remain in mainstream classrooms but are taken out for certain periods each week to be provided with intensive and, in my opinion, excellent instruction in some areas of reasoning and logic often known as "higher-order skills" in the contemporary jargon of the public schools. Children identified as "gifted" are admitted to this program in first grade and, in most cases, will remain there for six years. Even here, however, there are two tracks of the gifted. The regular gifted classes are provided with only one semester of this specialized instruction yearly. Those very few children, on the other hand, who are identified as showing the most promise are assigned, beginning in the third grade, to a program that receives a full-year regimen.

In one such class, containing ten intensely verbal and impressive fourth grade children, nine are white and one is Asian. The "special" class I enter first, by way of contrast, has twelve children of whom only one is white and none is Asian. These racial breakdowns prove to be predictive of the schoolwide pattern.

In a classroom for the gifted on the first floor of the school, I ask a child what the class is doing. "Logic and syllogisms," she replies. The room is fitted with a planetarium. The principal says that all the elementary schools in District 10 were given the same planetariums ten years ago but that certain schools, because of overcrowding, have been forced to give them up. At P.S. 261, according to my notes, there was a dome-like space that had been built to hold a planetarium, but the planetarium had been removed to free up space for the small library collection. P.S. 24, in contrast, has a spacious library that holds almost 8,000 books. The windows are decorated with attractive, brightly colored curtains and look out on flowering trees. The principal says that it's inadequate, but it appears spectacular to me after the cubicle that holds a meager 700 books within the former skating rink.

The district can't afford librarians, the principal says, but P.S. 24, unlike the poorer schools of District 10, can draw on educated parent volunteers who staff the room in shifts three days a week. A parent organization also raises independent funds to buy materials, including books, and will soon be running a fund-raiser to enhance the library's collection.

In a large and sunny first grade classroom that I enter next, I see 23 children, all of whom are white or Asian. In another first grade, there are 22 white children and two others who are Japanese. There is a computer in each class. Every classroom also has a modern fitted sink.

In a second grade class of 22 children, there are two black children and three Asian children. Again, there is a sink and a computer. A sixth grade social studies class has only one black child. The children have an in-class research area that holds some up-to-date resources. A set of encyclopedias (World Book, 1985) is in a rack beside a window. The children are doing a Spanish language lesson when I enter. Foreign languages begin in sixth grade at the school, but Spanish is offered also to the kindergarten children. As in every room at P.S. 24, the window shades are clean and new, the floor is neatly tiled in gray and green, and there is not a single light bulb missing.

Walking next into a special class, I see twelve children. One is white. Eleven are black. There are no Asian children. The room is half the size of mainstream classrooms. "Because of overcrowding," says the principal, "we have had to split these rooms in half." There is no computer and no sink.

I enter another special class. Of seven children, five are black, one is Hispanic, one is white. A little black boy with a large head sits in the far corner and is gazing at the ceiling.

"Placement of these kids," the principal explains, "can usually be traced to neurological damage."

In my notes: "How could so many of these children be brain-damaged?"

Next door to the special class is a woodworking shop. "This shop is only for the special classes," says the principal. The children learn to punch in time cards at the door, he says, in order to prepare them for employment.

The fourth grade gifted class, in which I spend the last part of the day, is humming with excitement. "I start with these children in the first grade," says the teacher. "We pull them out of mainstream classes on the basis of their test results and other factors such as the opinion of their teachers. Out of this group, beginning in third grade, I pull out the ones who show the most potential, and they enter classes such as this one."

The curriculum they follow, she explains, "emphasizes critical thinking, reasoning and logic." The planetarium, for instance, is employed not simply for the study of the universe as it exists. "Children also are designing their own galaxies," the teacher says.

A little girl sitting around a table with her classmates speaks with perfect poise: "My name is Susan. We are in the fourth grade gifted program."

I ask them what they're doing and a child says, "My name is Laurie and we're doing problem-solving."

A rather tall, good-natured boy who is half-standing at the table tells me that his name is David. "One thing that we do," he says, "is logical thinking. Some problems, we find, have more than one good answer. We need to learn not simply to be logical in our own thinking but to show respect for someone else's logic even when an answer may be technically incorrect."

When I ask him to explain this, he goes on, "A person who gives an answer that is not 'correct' may nonetheless have done some interesting thinking that we should examine. 'Wrong' answers may be more useful to examine than correct ones."

I ask the children if reasoning and logic are innate or if they're things that you can learn.

"You know some things to start with when you enter school," Susan says. "But we also learn some things that other children don't."

I ask her to explain this.

"We know certain things that other kids don't know because we're *taught* them."

She has braces on her teeth. Her long brown hair falls almost to her waist. Her loose white T-shirt has the word TRI-LOGIC on the front. She tells me that Tri-Logic is her father's firm.

Laurie elaborates on the same point: "Some things you know. Some kinds of logic are inside of you to start with. There are other things that someone needs to teach you."

David expands on what the other two have said: "Everyone can think and speak in logical ways unless they have a mental problem. What this program does is bring us to a higher form of logic."

The class is writing a new "Bill of Rights." The children already know the U.S. Bill of Rights and they explain its first four items to me with precision. What they are examining today, they tell me, is the very *concept* of a "right." Then they will create their own compendium of rights according to their own analysis and definition. Along one wall of the classroom, opposite the planetarium, are seven Apple II computers on which children have developed rather subtle color animations that express the themes—of greed and domination, for example—that they also have described in writing.

"This is an upwardly mobile group," the teacher later says. "They have exposure to whatever New York City has available. Their parents may take them to the theater, to museums...."

In my notes: "Six girls, four boys. Nine white, one Chinese. I am glad they have this class. But what about the others? Aren't there ten black children in the school who could enjoy this also?"

The teacher gives me a newspaper written, edited and computer-printed by her sixth grade gifted class. The children, she tells me, are provided with a link to kids in Europe for transmission of news stories.

A science story by one student asks if scientists have ever falsified their research. "Gregor Mendel," the sixth grader writes, "the Austrian monk who founded the science of genetics, published papers on his work with peas that some experts say were statistically too good to be true. Isaac Newton, who formulated the law of gravitation, relied on unseemly mathematical sleight of hand in his calculations.... Galileo Galilei, founder of modern scientific method, wrote about experiments that were so difficult to duplicate that colleagues doubted he had done them."

Another item in the paper, also by a sixth grade student, is less esoteric: "The Don Cossacks dance company, from Russia, is visiting the United States. The last time it toured America was 1976.... The Don Cossacks will be in New York City for two weeks at the Neil Simon Theater. Don't miss it!"

The tone is breezy—and so confident! That phrase—"Don't miss it!"—speaks a volume about life in Riverdale.

"What makes a good school?" asks the principal when we are talking later on. "The building and teachers are part of it, of course. But it isn't just the building and the teachers. Our kids come from good families and the neighborhood is good. In a three-block area we have a public library, a park, a junior high.... Our typical sixth grader reads at eighth grade level." In a quieter voice he says, "I see how hard my colleagues work in schools like P.S. 79. You have children in those neighborhoods who live in virtual hell. They enter school five years behind. What do they get?" Then, as he spreads his hands out on his desk, he says: "I have to ask myself why there should be an elementary school in District 10 with fifteen hundred children. Why should there be an elementary school within a skating rink? Why should the Board of Ed allow this? This is not the way that things should be."

———

Stark as the inequities in District 10 appear, educators say that they are "mild" in comparison to other situations in the city. Some of the most stunning inequality, according to a report by the Community Service Society, derives from allocations granted by state legislators to school districts where they have political allies. The poorest districts in the city get approximately 90 cents per pupil from these legislative grants, while the richest districts have been given $14 for each pupil.

Newspapers in New York City have reported other instances of the misallocation of resources. "The Board of Education," wrote the *New York Post* during July of 1987, "was hit with bombshell charges yesterday that money earmarked for fighting drug abuse and illiteracy in ghetto schools was funneled instead to schools in wealthy areas."

In receipt of extra legislative funds, according to the *Post*, affluent districts were funded "at a rate 14 times greater than low-income districts." The paper said the city's poorest areas were underfunded "with stunning consistency."

The report by the Community Service Society cites an official of the New York City Board of Education who remarks that there is "no point" in putting further money "into some poor districts" because, in his belief, "new teachers would not stay there." But the report observes that, in an instance where beginning teacher salaries were raised by nearly half, "that problem largely disappeared"—another interesting reminder of the difference money makes when we are willing to invest it. Nonetheless, says the report, "the perception that the poorest districts are beyond help still remains. . . ." Perhaps the worst result of such beliefs, says the report, is the message that resources would be "wasted on poor children." This message "trickles down to districts, schools, and classrooms." Children hear and understand this theme—they are poor investments—and behave accordingly. If society's resources would be wasted on their destinies, perhaps their own determination would be wasted too. "Expectations are a powerful force . . . ," the CSS observes.

Despite the evidence, the CSS report leans over backwards not to fuel the flames of racial indignation. "In the present climate," the report says, "suggestions of racism must be made with caution. However, it is inescapable that these inequities are being perpetrated on [school] districts which are virtually all black and Hispanic. . . ." While the report says, very carefully, that there is no "evidence" of "deliberate individual discrimination," it nonetheless concludes that "those who allocate resources make decisions over and over again which penalize the poorest districts." Analysis of city policy, the study says, "speaks to systemic bias which constitutes a conspiracy of effect. . . . Whether consciously or not, the system writes off its poorest students."

STUDY QUESTIONS

1. Why are the schools Kozol talks about so unequal? Why is there a distinct difference between the amount of money the poorer school has compared to the richer school?

2. The more affluent school couldn't afford a librarian, so how did they handle the librarian's duties? Why didn't the poorer schools use a similar solution? How else does the inequality between the schools go beyond the amount of money spent on each student?

3. Imagine that you attend the poor school described in the essay. Looking around the dilapidated building, what would you think **society** is trying to tell you about yourself?

4. The United States is the only industrialized nation that funds schools in the way that Kozol describes. How could officials make things more fair in your community and across the country? Research online how other countries distribute their educational resources and provide at least one example that you think would work well.

C. WRIGHT MILLS

The Power Elite

n this classic of **sociology**, C. Wright Mills (known for coining the term "the **sociological imagination**") exposes the systematic formation of the American **power elite**, its influence, and its prevalence in **society**. Although Mills wrote this piece in 1956, it remains current. Only the future will tell whether there will be a shift in the **power** structure or a continuation of the reach and influence of the power elite.

EXCEPT FOR THE UNSUCCESSFUL CIVIL WAR, CHANGES IN THE power system of the United States have not involved important challenges to its basic legitimations. Even when they have been decisive enough to be called "revolutions," they have not involved the "resort to the guns of a cruiser, the dispersal of an elected assembly by bayonets, or the mechanisms of a police state."[1] Nor have they involved, in any decisive way, any ideological struggle to control masses. Changes in the American structure of power have generally come about by institutional shifts in the relative positions of the political, the economic, and the military orders.

* * *

We study history, it has been said, to rid ourselves of it, and the history of the power elite is a clear case for which this maxim is correct. Like the tempo of American life in general, the long-term trends of the power structure have been greatly speeded up since World War II, and certain newer trends within and between the dominant

The Power Elite, 2nd Edition, by C. Wright Mills (1956). 4059 words from pp. 269, 274–278, 287–294, 296–297, 408–409. By permission of Oxford University Press, Inc.

[1] Cf. Elmer Davis, *But We Were Born Free* (Indianapolis: Bobbs-Merrill, 1953), p. 187.

institutions have also set the shape of the power elite and given historically specific meaning to its fifth epoch:

I. In so far as the structural clue to the power elite today lies in the political order, that clue is the decline of politics as genuine and public debate of alternative decisions— with nationally responsible and policy-coherent parties and with autonomous organizations connecting the lower and middle levels of power with the top levels of decision. America is now in considerable part more a formal political democracy than a democratic social structure, and even the formal political mechanics are weak.

The long-time tendency of business and government to become more intricately and deeply involved with each other has, in the fifth epoch, reached a new point of explicitness. The two cannot now be seen clearly as two distinct worlds. It is in terms of the executive agencies of the state that the rapprochement has proceeded most decisively. The growth of the executive branch of the government, with its agencies that patrol the complex economy, does not mean merely the "enlargement of government" as some sort of autonomous bureaucracy: it has meant the ascendancy of the corporation's man as a political eminence.

During the New Deal the corporate chieftains joined the political directorate; as of World War II they have come to dominate it. Long interlocked with government, now they have moved into quite full direction of the economy of the war effort and of the postwar era. This shift of the corporation executives into the political directorate has accelerated the long-term relegation of the professional politicians in the Congress to the middle levels of power.

II. In so far as the structural clue to the power elite today lies in the enlarged and military state, that clue becomes evident in the military ascendancy. The warlords have gained decisive political relevance, and the military structure of America is now in considerable part a political structure. The seemingly permanent military threat places a premium on the military and upon their control of men, materiel, money, and power; virtually all political and economic actions are now judged in terms of military definitions of reality: the higher warlords have ascended to a firm position within the power elite of the fifth epoch.

In part at least this has resulted from one simple historical fact, pivotal for the years since 1939: the focus of elite attention has been shifted from domestic problems, centered in the 'thirties around slump, to international problems, centered in the 'forties and 'fifties around war. Since the governing apparatus of the United States has by long historic usage been adapted to and shaped by domestic clash and balance, it has not, from any angle, had suitable agencies and traditions for the handling of international problems. Such formal democratic mechanics as had arisen in the century and a half of national development prior to 1941, had not been extended to the American handling of international affairs. It is, in considerable part, in this vacuum that the power elite has grown.

III. In so far as the structural clue to the power elite today lies in the economic order, that clue is the fact that the economy is at once a permanent-war economy and a private-corporation economy. American capitalism is now in considerable part a military capitalism, and the most important relation of the big corporation to the state rests on the coincidence of interests between military and corporate needs, as defined by warlords and corporate rich. Within the elite as a whole, this coincidence of interest between the high military and the corporate chieftains strengthens both of them and further subordinates the role of the merely political men. Not politicians, but corporate executives, sit with the military and plan the organization of war effort.

The shape and meaning of the power elite today can be understood only when these three sets of structural trends are seen at their point of coincidence: the military capitalism of private corporations exists in a weakened and formal democratic system containing a military order already quite political in outlook and demeanor. Accordingly, at the top of this structure, the power elite has been shaped by the coincidence of interest between those who control the major means of production and those who control the newly enlarged means of violence; from the decline of the professional politician and the rise to explicit political command of the corporate chieftains and the professional warlords; from the absence of any genuine civil service of skill and integrity, independent of vested interests.

The power elite is composed of political, economic, and military men, but this instituted elite is frequently in some tension: it comes together only on certain coinciding points and only on certain occasions of "crisis." In the long peace of the nineteenth century, the military were not in the high councils of state, not of the political directorate, and neither were the economic men—they made raids upon the state but they did not join its directorate. During the 'thirties, the political man was ascendant. Now the military and the corporate men are in top positions.

Of the three types of circle that compose the power elite today, it is the military that has benefited the most in its enhanced power, although the corporate circles have also become more explicitly intrenched in the more public decision-making circles. It is the professional politician that has lost the most, so much that in examining the events and decisions, one is tempted to speak of a political vacuum in which the corporate rich and the high warlord, in their coinciding interests, rule.

It should not be said that the three "take turns" in carrying the initiative, for the mechanics of the power elite are not often as deliberate as that would imply. At times, of course, it is—as when political men, thinking they can borrow the prestige of generals, find that they must pay for it, or, as when during big slumps, economic men feel the need of a politician at once safe and possessing vote appeal. Today all three are involved in virtually all widely ramifying decisions. Which of the three types seems to lead depends upon "the tasks of the period" as they, the elite, define them. Just now, these tasks center upon "defense" and international affairs. Accordingly, as we have seen, the military are ascendant in two senses: as personnel and as justifying ideology. That is why, just now, we can most easily specify the unity and the shape of the power elite in terms of the military ascendancy.

But we must always be historically specific and open to complexities. The simple Marxian view makes the big economic man the *real* holder of power; the simple liberal view makes the big political man the chief of the power system; and there are some who would view the warlords as virtual dictators. Each of these is an oversimplified view. It is to avoid them that we use the term "power elite" rather than, for example, "ruling class."[2]

In so far as the power elite has come to wide public attention, it has done so in terms of the "military clique." The power elite does, in fact, take its current shape from the decisive entrance into it of the military. Their presence and their ideology are its major legitimations, whenever the power elite feels the need to provide any. But what is called the "Washington military clique" is not composed merely of military men, and it does not prevail merely in Washington. Its members exist all over the country, and it is a coalition of generals in the roles of corporation executives, of politicians masquerading as admirals, of corporation executives acting like politicians, of civil servants who become majors, of vice-admirals who are also the assistants to a cabinet officer, who is himself, by the way, really a member of the managerial elite.

Neither the idea of a "ruling class" nor of a simple monolithic rise of "bureaucratic politicians" nor of a "military clique" is adequate. The power elite today involves the often uneasy coincidence of economic, military, and political power.

* * *

Despite their social similarity and psychological affinities, the members of the power elite do not constitute a club having a permanent membership with fixed and formal boundaries. It is of the nature of the power elite that within it there is a good

---

[2] "Ruling class" is a badly loaded phrase. "Class" is an economic term; "rule" a political one. The phrase, "ruling class," thus contains the theory that an economic class rules politically. That shortcut theory may or may not at times be true, but we do not want to carry that one rather simple theory about in the terms that we use to define our problems; we wish to state the theories explicitly, using terms of more precise and unilateral meaning. Specifically, the phrase "ruling class," in its common political connotations, does not allow enough autonomy to the political order and its agents, and it says nothing about the military as such. It should be clear to the reader by now that we do not accept as adequate the simple view that high economic men unilaterally make all decisions of national consequence. We hold that such a simple view of "economic determinism" must be elaborated by "political determinism" and "military determinism"; that the higher agents of each of these three domains now often have a noticeable degree of autonomy; and that only in the often intricate ways of coalition do they make up and carry through the most important decisions. Those are the major reasons we prefer "power elite" to "ruling class" as a characterizing phrase for the higher circles when we consider them in terms of power.

deal of shifting about, and that it thus does not consist of one small set of the same men in the same positions in the same hierarchies. Because men know each other personally does not mean that among them there is a unity of policy; and because they do not know each other personally does not mean that among them there is a disunity. The conception of the power elite does not rest, as I have repeatedly said, primarily upon personal friendship.

As the requirements of the top places in each of the major hierarchies become similar, the types of men occupying these roles at the top—by selection and by training in the jobs—become similar. This is no mere deduction from structure to personnel. That it is a fact is revealed by the heavy traffic that has been going on between the three structures, often in very intricate patterns. The chief executives, the warlords, and selected politicians came into contact with one another in an intimate, working way during World War II; after that war ended, they continued their associations, out of common beliefs, social congeniality, and coinciding interests. Noticeable proportions of top men from the military, the economic, and the political worlds have during the last fifteen years occupied positions in one or both of the other worlds: between these higher circles there is an interchangeability of position, based formally upon the supposed transferability of "executive ability," based in substances upon the co-optation by cliques of insiders. As members of a power elite, many of those busy in this traffic have come to look upon "the government" as an umbrella under whose authority they do their work.

As the business between the big three increases in volume and importance, so does the traffic in personnel. The very criteria for selecting men who will rise come to embody this fact. The corporate commissar, dealing with the state and its military, is wiser to choose a young man who has experienced the state and its military than one who has not. The political director, often dependent for his own political success upon corporate decisions and corporations, is also wiser to choose a man with corporate experience. Thus, by virtue of the very criterion of success, the interchange of personnel and the unity of the power elite is increased.

Given the formal similarity of the three hierarchies in which the several members of the elite spend their working lives, given the ramifications of the decisions made in each upon the others, given the coincidence of interest that prevails among them at many points, and given the administrative vacuum of the American civilian state along with its enlargement of tasks—given these trends of structure, and adding to them the psychological affinities we have noted—we should indeed be surprised were we to find that men said to be skilled in administrative contacts and full of organizing ability would fail to do more than get in touch with one another. They have, of course, done much more than that: increasingly, they assume positions in one another's domains.

The unity revealed by the interchangeability of top roles rests upon the parallel development of the top jobs in each of the big three domains. The interchange occurs most frequently at the points of their coinciding interest, as between regulatory agency and the regulated industry; contracting agency and contractor. And, as we shall see, it leads to co-ordinations that are more explicit, and even formal.

———————

The inner core of the power elite consists, first, of those who interchange commanding roles at the top of one dominant institutional order with those in another: the admiral who is also a banker and a lawyer and who heads up an important federal commission; the corporation executive whose company was one of the two or three leading war materiel producers who is now the Secretary of Defense; the wartime general who dons civilian clothes to sit on the political directorate and then becomes a member of the board of directors of a leading economic corporation.

Although the executive who becomes a general, the general who becomes a statesman, the statesman who becomes a banker, see much more than ordinary men in their ordinary environments, still the perspectives of even such men often remain tied to their dominant locales. In their very career, however, they interchange roles within the big three and thus readily transcend the particularity of interest in any one of these institutional milieux. By their very careers and activities, they lace the three types of milieux together. They are, accordingly, the core members of the power elite.

These men are not necessarily familiar with every major arena of power. We refer to one man who moves in and between perhaps two circles—say the industrial and the military—and to another man who moves in the military and the political, and to a third who moves in the political as well as among opinion-makers. These inbetween types most closely display our image of the power elite's structure and operation, even of behind-the-scenes operations. To the extent that there is any "invisible elite," these advisory and liaison types are its core. Even if—as I believe to be very likely—many of them are, at least in the first part of their careers, "agents" of the various elites rather than themselves elite, it is they who are most active in organizing the several top milieux into a structure of power and maintaining it.

The inner core of the power elite also includes men of the higher legal and financial type from the great law factories and investment firms, who are almost professional go-betweens of economic, political and military affairs, and who thus act to unify the power elite. The corporation lawyer and the investment banker perform the functions of the "go-between" effectively and powerfully. By the nature of their work, they transcend the narrower milieu of any one industry, and accordingly are in a position to speak and act for the corporate world or at least sizable sectors of it. The corporation lawyer is a key link between the economic and military and political areas; the investment banker is a key organizer and unifier of the corporate world and a person well versed in spending the huge amounts of money the American military establishment now ponders. When you get a lawyer who handles the legal work of investment bankers you get a key member of the power elite.

* * *

The outermost fringes of the power elite—which change more than its core—consist of "those who count" even though they may not be "in" on given decisions of consequence nor in their career move between the hierarchies. Each member of the power elite need not be a man who personally decides every decision that is to be ascribed to the power elite. Each member, in the decisions that he does make, takes the others seriously into account. They not only make decisions in the several major areas of war and peace; they are the men who, in decisions in which they take no direct part, are taken into decisive account by those who are directly in charge.

On the fringes and below them, somewhat to the side of the lower echelons, the power elite fades off into the middle levels of power, into the rank and file of the Congress, the pressure groups that are not vested in the power elite itself, as well as a multiplicity of regional and state and local interests. If all the men on the middle levels are not among those who count, they sometimes must be taken into account, handled, cajoled, broken or raised to higher circles.

* * *

The conception of the power elite and of its unity rests upon the corresponding developments and the coincidence of interests among economic, political, and military organizations. It also rests upon the similarity of origin and outlook, and the social and personal intermingling of the top circles from each of these dominant hierarchies. This conjunction of institutional and psychological forces, in turn, is revealed by the heavy personnel traffic within and between the big three institutional orders, as well as by the rise of go-betweens as in the high-level lobbying. The conception of the power elite, accordingly, does *not* rest upon the assumption that American history since the origins of World War II must be understood as a secret plot, or as a great and co-ordinated conspiracy of the members of this elite. The conception rests upon quite impersonal grounds.

There is, however, little doubt that the American power elite—which contains, we are told, some of "the greatest organizers in the world"—has also planned and has plotted. The rise of the elite, as we have already made clear, was not and could not have been caused by a plot; and the tenability of the conception does not rest upon the existence of any secret or any publicly known organization. But, once the conjunction of structural trend and of the personal will to utilize it gave rise to the power elite, then plans and programs did occur to its members and indeed it is not possible to interpret many events and official policies of the fifth epoch without reference to the power elite. "There is a great difference," Richard Hofstadter has remarked, "between locating conspiracies *in* history and saying that history *is*, in effect, a conspiracy..."[2]

The structural trends of institutions become defined as opportunities by those who occupy their command posts. Once such opportunities are recognized, men may avail themselves of them. Certain types of men from each of the dominant institutional areas, more far-sighted than others, have actively promoted the liaison before it took its truly modern shape. They have often done so for reasons not shared by their partners, although not objected to by them either; and often the outcome of their liaison has had consequences which none of them foresaw, much less shaped, and which only later in the course of development came under explicit control. Only after it was well under way did most of its members find themselves part of it and become gladdened, although sometimes also worried, by this fact. But once the co-ordination is a going concern, new men come readily into it and assume its existence without question.

So far as explicit organization—conspiratorial or not—is concerned, the power elite, by its very nature, is more likely to use existing organizations, working within and between them, than to set up explicit organizations whose membership is strictly limited to its own members. But if there is no machinery in existence to ensure, for example, that military and political factors will be balanced in decisions made, they will invent such machinery and use it, as with the National Security Council. Moreover, in a formally democratic polity, the aims and the powers of the various elements of this elite are further supported by an aspect of the permanent war economy: the assumption that the security of the nation supposedly rests upon great secrecy of plan and intent. Many higher events that would reveal the working of the power elite can be withheld from public knowledge under the guise of secrecy. With the wide secrecy covering their operations and decisions, the power elite can mask their intentions, operations, and further consolidation. Any secrecy that is imposed upon those in positions to observe high decision-makers clearly works for and not against the operations of the power elite.

There is accordingly reason to suspect—but by the nature of the case, no proof—that the power elite is not altogether "surfaced." There is nothing hidden about it, although its activities are not publicized. As an elite, it is not organized, although its members often know one another, seem quite naturally to work together, and share many organizations in common. There is nothing conspiratorial about it, although its decisions are often publicly unknown and its mode of operation manipulative rather than explicit.

It is not that the elite "believe in" a compact elite behind the scenes and a mass down below. It is not put in that language. It is just that the people are of necessity confused and must, like trusting children, place all the new world of foreign policy and strategy and executive action in the hands of experts. It is just that everyone knows somebody has got to run the show, and that somebody usually does. Others do not really care anyway, and besides, they do not know how. So the gap between the two types gets wider.

* * *

The idea of the power elite rests upon and enables us to make sense of (1) the decisive institutional trends that characterize the structure of our epoch, in particular, the military ascendancy in a privately incorporated economy, and more broadly, the several coincidences of objective interests between economic, military, and political institutions; (2) the social similarities and the psychological affinities of the men who occupy the command posts of these structures, in particular the increased interchangeability of the top positions in each of them and the increased traffic between these orders in the careers of men of power; (3) the ramifications, to the point of virtual totality, of the kind of decisions that are made at the top, and the rise to power of a set of men who, by training and bent, are professional organizers of considerable force and who are unrestrained by democratic party training.

Negatively, the formation of the power elite rests upon (1) the relegation of the professional party politician to the middle levels of power, (2) the semi-organized stalemate of the interests of sovereign localities into which the legislative function has fallen, (3) the virtually complete absence of a civil service that constitutes a politically neutral, but politically relevant, depository of brainpower and executive skill, and (4) the increased official secrecy behind which great decisions are made without benefit of public or even Congressional debate.

As a result, the political directorate, the corporate rich, and the ascendant military have come together as the power elite, and the expanded and centralized hierarchies which they head have encroached upon the old balances and have now relegated them to the middle levels of power. Now the balancing society is a conception that pertains accurately to the middle levels, and on that level the balance has become more often an affair of intrenched provincial and nationally irresponsible forces and demands than a center of power and national decision.

But how about the bottom? As all these trends have become visible at the top and on the middle, what has been happening to the great American public? If the top is unprecedentedly powerful and increasingly unified and willful; if the middle zones are increasingly a semi-organized stalemate—in what shape is the bottom, in what condition is the public at large? The rise of the power elite, we shall now see, rests upon, and in some ways is part of, the transformation of the publics of America into a mass society.

STUDY QUESTIONS

1. What does Mills mean by the **power elite**?

2. What are the three domains of the power elite? Describe the interests of the power elite.

3. Identify two nationally elected officials, research what positions they held before serving their terms, what decisions they made during their time in office, and what positions they took after their public service. Discuss your results and whether they are evidence of the continued existence of the power elite.

4. Watch the documentary *Inside Job* and discuss current examples of the power elite. If the power elite lost **power**, would they be replaced? By whom?

JEAN KILBOURNE

"The More You Subtract, the More You Add": Cutting Girls Down to Size

from Deadly Persuasion: Why Women and Girls Must Fight the Addictive Power of Advertising

Ideal women should be small, quiet, and pretty. They should be both virginal and sexy—or at least that's the message we can get from the misogynistic and offensive messages that pervade our **society**. In "The More You Subtract, the More You Add," Jean Kilbourne takes a closer look at the advertising and **media** industries to see what messages young men and women are given about what it means to be feminine.

WHEN I WAS SIXTEEN, LIKE ALMOST EVERYONE ELSE IN THE world, I fell wildly in love for the first time. My feelings were so intense that now, decades later, I still dream about him from time to time. He was good for me in every way, but I also began a sinister love affair around the same time, one that nearly consumed me—my love affair with alcohol and cigarettes. As adults in a toxic culture, some of us fall in love with cars or chocolate cake or, more dangerously, drugs. But, just as we are more vulnerable to the glory and heartbreak of romantic love than we will ever be again, at no time are we more vulnerable to the seductive power of advertising and of addiction than we are in adolescence.

Adolescents are new and inexperienced consumers—and such prime targets. They are in the process of learning their values and roles and developing their self-concepts.

Most teenagers are sensitive to peer pressure and find it difficult to resist or even to question the dominant cultural messages perpetuated and reinforced by the media. Mass communication has made possible a kind of national peer pressure that erodes private and individual values and standards, as well as community values and standards. As Margaret Mead once said, today our children are not brought up by parents, they are brought up by the mass media.

Advertisers are aware of their role and do not hesitate to take advantage of the insecurities and anxieties of young people, usually in the guise of offering solutions. A cigarette provides a symbol of independence. A pair of designer jeans or sneakers convey status. The right perfume or beer resolves doubts about femininity or masculinity. All young people are vulnerable to these messages and adolescence is a difficult time for most people, perhaps especially these days. According to the Carnegie Corporation, "Nearly half of all American adolescents are at high or moderate risk of seriously damaging their life chances." But there is a particular kind of suffering in our culture that afflicts girls.

As most of us know so well by now, when a girl enters adolescence, she faces a series of losses—loss of self-confidence, loss of a sense of efficacy and ambition, and the loss of her "voice," the sense of being a unique and powerful self that she had in childhood. Girls who were active, confident, feisty at the ages of eight and nine and ten often become hesitant, insecure, self-doubting at eleven. Their self-esteem plummets. As Carol Gilligan, Mary Pipher and other social critics and psychologists have pointed out in recent years, adolescent girls in America are afflicted with a range of problems, including low self-esteem, eating disorders, binge drinking, date rape and other dating violence, teen pregnancy, and a rise in cigarette smoking. Teenage women today are engaging in far riskier health behavior in greater numbers than any prior generation.

The gap between boys and girls is closing, but this is not always for the best. According to a 1998 status report by a consortium of universities and research centers, girls have closed the gap with boys in math performance and are coming close in science. But they are also now smoking, drinking, and using drugs as often as boys their own age. And, although girls are not nearly as violent as boys, they are committing more crimes than ever before and are far more often physically attacking each other.

It is important to understand that these problems go way beyond individual psychological development and pathology. Even girls who are raised in loving homes by supportive parents grow up in a toxic cultural environment, at risk for self-mutilation, eating disorders, and addictions. The culture, both reflected and reinforced by advertising, urges girls to adopt a false self, to bury alive their real selves, to become "feminine," which means to be nice and kind and sweet, to compete with other girls for the attention of boys, and to value romantic relationships with boys above all else. Girls are put into a terrible double bind. They are supposed to repress their power, their anger, their exuberance and be simply "nice," although they also eventually must compete with men in the business world and be successful. They must be overtly sexy and attractive but essentially passive and virginal. It is not surprising that most girls experience this time as painful and confusing, especially if they are unconscious of these conflicting demands.

Of course, it is impossible to speak accurately of girls as a monolithic group. The socialization that emphasizes passivity and compliance does not apply to many African-American and Jewish girls, who are often encouraged to be assertive and outspoken, and working-class girls are usually not expected to be stars in the business world. Far from protecting these girls from eating disorders and other problems, these differences more often mean that the problems remain hidden or undiagnosed and the girls are even less likely to get help. Eating problems affect girls from African-American, Asian, Native American, Hispanic, and Latino families and from every socioeconomic background. The racism and classism that these girls experience exacerbate their problems. Sexism is by no means the only trauma they face.

* * *

Girls try to make sense of the contradictory expectations of themselves in a culture dominated by advertising. Advertising is one of the most potent messengers in a culture that can be toxic for girls' self-esteem. Indeed, if we looked only at advertising images, this would be a bleak world for females. Girls are extremely desirable to advertisers because they are new consumers, are beginning to have significant disposable income, and are developing brand loyalty that might last a lifetime. Teenage girls spend over $4 billion annually on cosmetics alone.

Seventeen, a magazine aimed at girls about twelve to fifteen, sells these girls to advertisers in an ad that says, "She's the one you want. She's the one we've got." The copy continues, "She pursues beauty and fashion at every turn" and concludes with, "It's more than a magazine. It's her life." In another similar ad, *Seventeen* refers to itself as a girl's "Bible." Many girls read magazines like this and take the advice seriously. Regardless of the intent of the advertisers, what are the messages that girls are getting? What are they told?

Primarily girls are told by advertisers that what is most important about them is their perfume, their clothing, their bodies, their beauty. Their "essence" is their underwear. "He says the first thing he noticed about you is your great personality," says an ad featuring a very young woman in tight jeans. The copy continues, "He lies." "If this is your idea of a great catch," says an ad for a cosmetic kit from a teen magazine featuring a cute boy, "this is your tackle box." Even very little girls are offered makeup and toys like Special Night Barbie, which shows them how to dress up for a night out. Girls of all ages get the message that they must be flawlessly beautiful and, above all these days, they must be thin.

Even more destructively, they get the message that this is possible, that, with enough effort and self-sacrifice, they can achieve this ideal. Thus many girls spend enormous amounts of time and energy attempting to achieve something that is not only trivial but also completely unattainable. The glossy images of flawlessly beautiful and extremely thin women that surround us would not have the impact they do if we did not live in a culture that encourages us to believe we can and should remake our bodies into perfect commodities. These images play into the American belief of transformation and ever-new possibilities, no longer via hard work but via the purchase of the right products. As Anne Becker has pointed out, this belief is by no means universal. People in many other cultures may admire a particular body shape without seeking to emulate it. In the Western world, however, "the anxiety of nonrecognition ('I don't fit in') faced by the majority of spectators is more often translated into identifications ('I want to be like that') and attempts at self-alteration than into rage."

Women are especially vulnerable because our bodies have been objectified and commodified for so long. And young women are the most vulnerable, especially those who have experienced early deprivation, sexual abuse, family violence, or other trauma. Cultivating a thinner body offers some hope of control and success to a young woman with a poor self-image and overwhelming personal problems that have no easy solutions.

Although troubled young women are especially vulnerable, these messages affect all girls. A researcher at Brigham and Women's Hospital in Boston found that the more frequently girls read magazines, the more likely they were to diet and to feel that magazines influence their ideal body shape. Nearly half reported wanting to lose weight because of a magazine picture (but only 29 percent were actually overweight). Studies at Stanford University and the University of Massachusetts found that about 70 percent of college women say they feel worse about their own looks after reading women's magazines. Another study, this one of 350 young men and women, found that a preoccupation with one's appearance takes a toll on mental health. Women scored much higher than men on what the researchers called "self-objectification." This tendency to view one's body from the outside in—regarding physical attractiveness, sex appeal, measurements, and weight as more central to one's physical identity than health, strength, energy level, coordination, or fitness—has many harmful effects, including diminished mental performance, increased feelings of shame and anxiety, depression, sexual dysfunction, and the development of eating disorders.

These images of women seem to affect men most strikingly by influencing how they judge the real women in their lives. Male college students who viewed just one episode of *Charlie's Angels*, the hit television show of the 1970s that featured three beautiful women, were harsher in their evaluations of the attractiveness of potential dates than were males who had not seen the episode. In another study, male college students shown centerfolds from *Playboy* and *Penthouse* were more likely to find their own girlfriends less sexually attractive.

Adolescent girls are especially vulnerable to the obsession with thinness, for many reasons. One is the ominous peer pressure on young people. Adolescence is a time of such self-consciousness and terror of shame and humiliation. Boys are shamed for being too small, too "weak," too soft, too sensitive. And girls are shamed for being too sexual, too loud, too boisterous, too big (in any sense of the word), having too hearty an appetite. Many young women have told me that their boyfriends wanted them to lose weight. One said that her boyfriend had threatened to leave her if she didn't lose five pounds. "Why don't you leave him," I asked, "and lose 160?"

The situation is very different for men. The double standard is reflected in an ad for a low-fat pizza: "He eats a brownie . . . you eat a rice cake. He eats a juicy burger . . . you eat a low fat entree. He eats pizza . . . you eat pizza. Finally, life is fair." Although some men develop eating problems, the predominant cultural message remains that a hearty appetite and a large size is desirable in a man, but not so in a woman.

Indeed, a 1997 television campaign targets ravenous teenage boys by offering Taco Bell as the remedy for hunger (and also linking eating with sex via the slogan "Want some?"). One commercial features a fat guy who loses his composure when he realizes his refrigerator is empty. In another, two quite heavy guys have dozed off in front of a television set and are awakened by hunger pangs, which only Taco Bell can satisfy. It is impossible to imagine this campaign aimed at teenage girls.

Normal physiological changes during adolescence result in increased body fat for women. If these normal changes are considered undesirable by the culture (and by parents and peers), this can lead to chronic anxiety and concern about weight control in young women. A ten-year-old girl wrote to *New Moon*, a feminist magazine for girls, "I was at the beach and was in my bathing suit. I have kind of fat legs, and my uncle told me I had fat legs in front of all my cousins and my cousins' friends. I was so embarrassed, I went up to my room and shut the door. When I went downstairs again, everyone started teasing me." Young women are even encouraged to worry about small fluctuations in their weight. "Sometimes what you wear to dinner may depend on what you eat for breakfast," says an ad for cereal that pictures a slinky black dress. In truth, daily and weekly and monthly fluctuations in weight are perfectly normal.

The obsession starts early. Some studies have found that from 40 to 80 percent of fourth-grade girls are dieting. Today at least one-third of twelve- to thirteen-year-old girls are actively trying to lose weight, by dieting, vomiting, using laxatives, or taking diet pills. One survey found that 63 percent of high-school girls were on diets, compared with only 16 percent of men. And a survey in Massachusetts found that the single largest group of high-school students considering or attempting suicide are girls who feel they are overweight. Imagine. Girls made to feel so terrible about themselves that they would rather be dead than fat. This wouldn't be happening, of course, if it weren't for our last "socially acceptable" prejudice—weightism. Fat children are ostracized and ridiculed from the moment they enter school, and fat adults, women in particular, are subjected to public contempt and scorn. This strikes terror into the hearts of all women, many of whom, unfortunately, identify with the oppressor and become vicious to themselves and each other.

No wonder it is hard to find a woman, especially a young woman, in America today who has a truly healthy attitude toward her body and toward food. Just as the disease of alcoholism is the extreme end of a continuum that includes a wide range of alcohol use and abuse, so are bulimia and anorexia the extreme results of an obsession with eating and weight control that grips many young women with serious and potentially very dangerous results. Although eating problems are often thought to result from vanity, the truth is that they, like other addictions and compulsive behavior, usually have deeper roots—not only genetic predisposition and biochemical vulnerabilities, but also childhood sexual abuse.

Advertising doesn't cause eating problems, of course, any more than it causes alcoholism. Anorexia in particular is a disease with a complicated etiology, and media images probably don't play a major role. However, these images certainly contribute to the body-hatred so many young women feel and to some of the resulting eating problems, which range from bulimia to compulsive overeating to simply being obsessed with controlling one's appetite. Advertising does promote abusive and abnormal attitudes about eating, drinking, and thinness. It thus provides fertile soil for these obsessions to take root in and creates a climate of denial in which these diseases flourish.

The influence of the media is strikingly illustrated in a recent study that found a sharp rise in eating disorders among young women in Fiji soon after the introduction of television to the culture. Before television was available, there was little talk of dieting in Fiji. "You've gained weight" was a traditional compliment and "going thin" the sign of a problem. In 1995 television came to the island. Within three years, the number of teenagers at risk for eating disorders more than doubled, 74 percent of the teens in the study said they felt "too big or too fat," and 62 percent said they had dieted in the past month. Of course, this doesn't prove a direct causal link between television and eating disorders. Fiji is a culture in transition in many ways. However, it seems more than coincidental that the Fiji girls who were heavy viewers of television were 50 percent more likely to describe themselves as fat and 30 percent more likely to diet than those girls who watched television less frequently. As Ellen Goodman says, "The big success story of our entertainment industry is our ability to export insecurity: We can make any woman anywhere feel perfectly rotten about her shape."

Being obsessed about one's weight is made to seem normal and even appealing in ads for unrelated products, such as a scotch ad that features a very thin and pretty young woman looking in a mirror while her boyfriend observes her. The copy, addressed to him, says, "Listen, if you can handle 'Honey, do I look fat?' you can handle this." These two are so intimate that she can share her deepest fears with him—and he can respond by chuckling at her adorable vulnerability and knocking back another scotch. And everyone who sees the ad gets the message that it is perfectly normal for all young women, including thin and attractive ones, to worry about their weight.

"Put some weight on," says a British ad featuring an extremely thin young woman—but the ad is referring to her watch. She is so thin she can wear the watch on her upper arm—and this is supposed to be a good thing.

Not all of this is intentional on the part of the advertisers, of course. A great deal of it *is* based on research and *is* intended to arouse anxiety and affect women's self-esteem. But some of it reflects the unconscious attitudes and beliefs of the individual advertisers, as well as what Carl Jung referred to as the "collective unconscious." Advertisers are members of the culture too and have been as thoroughly conditioned as anyone else. The magazines and the ads deliberately *create* and intensify anxiety about weight because it is so profitable. On a deeper level, however, they *reflect* cultural concerns and conflicts about women's power. Real freedom for women would change the very basis of our male-dominated society. It is not surprising that many men (and women, to be sure) fear this.

"The more you subtract, the more you add," says an ad that ran in several women's and teen magazines in 1997. Surprisingly, it is an ad for clothing, not for a diet product. Overtly, it is a statement about minimalism in fashion. However, the fact that the girl in the ad is very young and very thin reinforces another message, a message that an adolescent girl constantly gets from advertising and throughout the popular culture, the message that she should diminish herself, she should be *less* than she is.

On the most obvious and familiar level, this refers to her body. However, the loss, the subtraction, the cutting down to size also refers to her sense of her self, her sexuality, her need for authentic connection, and her longing for power and freedom. I certainly don't think that the creators of this particular ad had all this in mind. They're simply selling expensive clothing in an unoriginal way, by using a very young and very thin woman—and an unfortunate tagline. It wouldn't be important at all were there not so many other ads that reinforce this message and did it not coincide with a cultural crisis taking place now for adolescent girls.

"We cut Judy down to size," says an ad for a health club. "Soon, you'll both be taking up less space," says an ad for a collapsible treadmill, referring both to the product and to the young woman exercising on it. *The obsession with thinness is most deeply about cutting girls and women down to size.* It is only a symbol, albeit a very powerful and destructive one, of tremendous fear of female power. Powerful women are seen by many people (women as well as men) as inherently destructive and dangerous. Some argue that it is men's awareness of just how powerful women can be that has created the attempts to keep women small. Indeed, thinness as an ideal has always accompanied periods of greater freedom for women—as soon as we got the vote, boyish flapper bodies came into vogue. No wonder there is such pressure on young women today to be thin, to shrink, to be like little girls, not to take up too much space, literally or figuratively.

At the same time there is relentless pressure on women to be small, there is also pressure on us to succeed, to achieve, to "have it all." We can be successful as long as we stay "feminine" (i.e., powerless enough not to be truly threatening). One way to do this is to present an image of fragility, to look like a waif. This demonstrates that one is both in control and still very "feminine." One of the many double binds tormenting young women today is the need to be both sophisticated and accomplished, yet also delicate and childlike. Again, this applies mostly to middle- to upper-class white women.

The changing roles and greater opportunities for women promised by the women's movement are trivialized, reduced to the private search for the slimmest body. In one commercial, three skinny young women dance and sing about the "taste of freedom." They are feeling free because they can now eat bread, thanks to a low-calorie version. A commercial for a fast-food chain features a very slim young woman who announces, "I have a license to eat." The salad bar and lighter fare have given her freedom to eat (as if eating for women were a privilege rather than a need). "Free yourself," says ad after ad for diet products.

You can never be too rich or too thin, girls are told. This mass delusion sells a lot of products. It also causes enormous suffering, involving girls in false quests for power and control, while deflecting attention and energy from that which might really empower them. "A declaration of independence," proclaims an ad for perfume that features an emaciated model, but in fact the quest for a body as thin as the model's becomes a prison for many women and girls.

The quest for independence can be a problem too if it leads girls to deny the importance of and need for interpersonal relationships. Girls and young women today are encouraged by the culture to achieve a very "masculine" kind of autonomy and independence, one that excludes interdependence, mutuality, and connection with others. Catherine Steiner-Adair suggests that perhaps eating disorders emerge at adolescence because it is at this point that "females experience themselves to be at a crossroads in their lives where they must shift from a relational approach to life to an autonomous one, a shift that can represent an intolerable loss when independence is associated with isolation." In this sense, she sees eating disorders as political statements, a kind of hunger strike: "Girls with eating disorders have a heightened, albeit confused, grasp of the dangerous imbalance of the culture's values, which they cannot articulate in the face of the culture's abject denial of their adolescent intuitive truth, so they tell their story with their bodies."

Most of us know by now about the damage done to girls by the tyranny of the ideal image, weightism, and the obsession with thinness. But girls get other messages too that "cut them down to size" more subtly. In ad after ad girls are urged to be "barely there"—beautiful but silent. Of course, girls are not just influenced by images of other girls. They are even more powerfully attuned to images of women, because they learn from these images what is expected of them, what they are to become. And they see these images again and again in the magazines they read, even those magazines designed for teenagers, and in the commercials they watch.

"Make a statement without saying a word," says an ad for perfume. And indeed this is one of the primary messages of the culture to adolescent girls. "The silence of a look can reveal more than words," says another perfume ad, this one featuring a woman lying on her back. "More than words can say," says yet another perfume ad, and a clothing ad says, "Classic is speaking your mind (without saying a word)." An ad for lipstick says, "Watch your mouth, young lady," while one for nail polish says, "Let your fingers do the talking," and one for hairspray promises "hair that speaks volumes." In another ad, a young woman's turtleneck is pulled over her mouth. And an ad for a movie soundtrack features a chilling image of a young woman with her lips sewn together.

It is not only the girls themselves who see these images, of course. Their parents and teachers and doctors see them and they influence their sense of how girls should be. A 1999 study done at the University of Michigan found that, beginning in pre-school, girls are told to be quiet much more often than boys. Although boys were much noisier than girls, the girls were told to speak softly or to use a "nicer" voice about three times more often. Girls were encouraged to be quiet, small, and physically constrained. The researcher concluded that one of the consequences of this socialization is that girls grow into women afraid to speak up for themselves or to use their voices to protect themselves from a variety of dangers.

A television commercial features a very young woman lying on a bed, giggling, silly. Suddenly a male hand comes forward. His finger touches her lips and she becomes silent, her face blank. Another commercial features a very young woman, shot in black and white but with colored contact lenses. She never speaks but she touches her face and her hair as a female voiceover says, "Your eyes don't just see, they also speak... Your eyes can say a lot, but they don't have to shout. They can speak softly. Let your eyes be heard... without making a sound." The commercial ends with the young woman putting her finger in her mouth.

"Score high on nonverbal skills," says a clothing ad featuring a young African-American woman, while an ad for mascara tells young women to "make up your own language." And an Italian ad features a very thin young woman in an elegant coat sitting on a window seat. The copy says, "This woman is silent. This coat talks." Girls, seeing these images of women, are encouraged to be silent, mysterious, not to talk too much or too loudly. In many different ways, they are told "the more you subtract, the more you add." In this kind of climate, a Buffalo jeans ad featuring a young woman screaming, "I don't have to scream for attention but I do," can seem like an improvement—until we notice that she's really getting attention by unbuttoning her blouse to her navel. This is typical of the mixed messages so many ads and other forms of the media give girls. The young woman seems fierce and powerful, but she's really exposed, vulnerable.

The January 1998 cover of *Seventeen* highlights an article, "Do you talk too much?" On the back cover is an ad for Express mascara, which promises "high voltage volume instantly!" As if the way that girls can express themselves and turn up the volume is via their mascara. Is this harmless wordplay, or is it a sophisticated and clever marketing ploy based on research about the silencing of girls, deliberately designed to attract them with the promise of at least some form of self-expression? Advertisers certainly spend a lot of money on psychological research and focus groups. I would expect these groups to reveal, among other things, that teenage girls are angry but reticent. Certainly the cumulative effect of these images and words urging girls to express themselves only through their bodies and through products is serious and harmful.

Many ads feature girls and young women in very passive poses, limp, doll-like, sometimes acting like little girls, playing with dolls and wearing bows in their hair. One ad uses a pacifier to sell lipstick and another the image of a baby to sell BabyDoll Blush Highlight. "Lolita seems to be a comeback kid," says a fashion layout featuring a woman wearing a ridiculous hairstyle and a baby-doll dress, standing with shoulders slumped and feet apart. In women's and teen magazines it is virtually impossible to tell the fashion layouts from the ads. Indeed, they exist to support each other.

As Erving Goffman pointed out in *Gender Advertisements*, we learn a great deal about the disparate power of males and females simply through the body language and poses of advertising. Women, especially young women, are generally subservient to men in ads, through both size and position. Sometimes it is as blatant as the woman serving as a footrest in the ad for Think Skateboards.

Other times, it is more subtle but quite striking (once one becomes aware of it). The double-paged spread for Calvin Klein's clothing for kids conveys a world of information about the relative power of boys and girls. One of the boys seems to be in the act of speaking, expressing himself, while the girl has her hand over her mouth. Boys are generally shown in ads as active, rambunctious, while girls are more often passive and focused on their appearance. The exception to the rule involves African-American children, male and female, who are often shown in advertising as passive observers of their white playmates.

That these stereotypes continue, in spite of all the recent focus on the harm done to girls by enforced passivity, is evident in the most casual glance at parents' magazines. In the ads in the March 1999 issues of *Child* and *Parents*, all of the boys are active and all of the girls are passive. In *Child*, a boy plays on the jungle gym in one ad, while in another, a girl stands quietly, looking down, holding some flowers. In *Parents*, a boy rides a bike, full of excitement, while a girl is happy about having put on lipstick. It's hard to believe that this is 1999 and not 1959. The more things change, the more they stay the same.

Girls are often shown as playful clowns in ads, perpetuating the attitude that girls and women are childish and cannot be taken seriously, whereas even very young men are generally portrayed as secure, powerful, and serious. People in control of their lives stand upright, alert, and ready to meet the world. In contrast, females often appear off-balance, insecure, and weak. Often our body parts are bent, conveying unpreparedness, submissiveness, and appeasement. We exhibit what Goffman terms "licensed withdrawal"—seeming to be psychologically removed, disoriented, defenseless, spaced out.

Females touch people and things delicately, we caress, whereas males grip, clench, and grasp. We cover our faces with our hair or our hands, conveying shame or embarrassment. And, no matter what happens, we keep on smiling. "Just smiling the bothers away," as one ad says. This ad is particularly disturbing because the model is a young African-American woman, a member of a group that has long been encouraged to just keep smiling, no matter what. She's even wearing a kerchief, like Aunt Jemima. The cultural fear of angry women is intensified dramatically when the women are African-American.

An extreme example of the shaming and trivialization of girls and women is a recent little trend of ads featuring young women sitting on the toilet, such as the shoe ad with popular MTV star Jenny McCarthy (although the ad offended a lot of people, it also boosted sales of Candies shoes by 19 percent). Unfortunately, this phenomenon is not restricted to the United States. An Italian ad for sneakers and a British one for a magazine use the same image. Such pictures are especially humiliating to self-conscious teenagers.

Girls and young women are often presented as blank and fragile. Floating in space, adrift in a snowstorm. A Valentino clothing ad perhaps unwittingly illustrates the tragedy of adolescence for girls. It features a very young woman with her head seemingly enclosed in a glass bubble labeled "Love." Some ads and fashion layouts picture girls as mermaids or underwater as if they were drowning—or lying on the ground as if washed up to shore, such as the Versace makeup ad picturing a young girl caught up in fishing nets, rope, and seashells. An ad for vodka features a woman in the water and the copy, "In a past life I was a mermaid who fell in love with an ancient mariner. I pulled him into the sea to be my husband. I didn't know he couldn't breathe underwater." Of course, she can't breathe underwater either.

Breathe underwater. As girls come of age sexually, the culture gives them impossibly contradictory messages. As the *Seventeen* ad says, "She wants to be outrageous. And accepted." Advertising slogans such as "because innocence is sexier than you think," "Purity, yes. Innocence never," and "nothing so sensual was ever so innocent" place them in a double bind. "Only something so pure could inspire such unspeakable passion," declares an ad for Jovan musk that features a white flower. Somehow girls are supposed to be both innocent and seductive, virginal and experienced, all at the same time. As they quickly learn, this is tricky.

Females have long been divided into virgins and whores, of course. What is new is that girls are now supposed to embody both within themselves. This is symbolic of the central contradiction of the culture—we must work hard and produce and achieve success and yet, at the same time, we are encouraged to live impulsively, spend a lot of money, and be constantly and immediately gratified. This tension is reflected in our attitudes toward many things, including sex and eating. Girls are promised fulfillment both through being thin and through eating rich foods, just as they are promised fulfillment through being innocent and virginal and through wild and impulsive sex.

Young people, boys and girls, are surrounded by messages urging them to be sexually active. Teachers report a steady escalation of sex talk among children, starting in *preschool*, as our children are prematurely exposed to a barrage of sexual information and misinformation through advertising, television shows, music, and films. "You can learn more about anatomy after school," says an ad for jeans, which manages to trivialize sex, relationships, and education all in one sentence.

The consequences of all this sexual pressure on children are frightening. The average age of first sexual intercourse is about sixteen for girls and fifteen for boys. Far more disturbing is the fact that seven in ten girls who had sex before the age of fourteen and six in ten of those who had sex before the age of fifteen report having sex involuntarily. One of every ten girls under the age of twenty becomes pregnant in the United States each year, more than in any other industrialized country in the world: twice as high as in England and Wales, France and Canada, and nine times as high as in the Netherlands or Japan. And as many as one in six sexually active adolescents has a sexually transmitted disease.

Of course, advertising and the media are not solely to blame for these appalling statistics. But they are the leading source of sex education in the nation and they create a climate which encourages a very cavalier attitude toward sex. The typical teenage viewer who watches an average of three to five hours of television a day sees a minimum of two thousand sexual acts per year on television alone. There is also abundant sexual activity, of course, in music videos, books, movies, cartoons, video games, and song lyrics aimed at teenagers, almost all of it portraying sexual behavior as consequence-free and much of it exploiting women's bodies and glamorizing sexual violence. Magazines targeting girls and young women are filled with ads and articles on how to be beautiful and sexy and appealing to boys—all in service of the advertisers, of course, who sell their wares on almost every page. "How Smart Girls Flirt," "Sex to Write Home About," "15 Ways Sex Makes You Prettier," and "Are You Good in Bed?" are some of the cover stories for a teen magazine called *Jane*.

At the same time, there is rarely any accurate information about sex (the networks still refuse to run condom ads) and certainly never any emphasis on relationships or intimacy (there is hardly time in thirty seconds for the sexual encounter, let alone any development of character!). We have to fight to get sex education into our schools, and the government refuses to fund any program that doesn't insist on abstinence as the only choice suitable for young people (how quickly people forget their own adolescence). Young people learn in school and in church that sex can hurt or kill them, but not that it can bring pleasure, joy, and connection. How can they learn to say "Yes!" in a loving and responsible way?

It is difficult to do the kind of research that would prove the effects of the media on sexual attitudes and behavior—because of the perceived sensitivity of sex as a topic and because of the difficulty in finding a comparison group. However, the few existing studies consistently point to a relationship between exposure to sexual content and sexual beliefs, attitudes, and behavior. Two studies have found correlations between watching higher doses of "sexy" television and early initiation of sexual intercourse, and studies of adolescents have found that heavy television viewing is predictive of negative attitudes toward virginity. In general, key communication theories and years of research on other kinds of communications effects, such as the effect of violent images, suggest that we are indeed affected by the ubiquitous, graphic, and consequence-free depictions of sexual behavior that surround us in all forms of the mass media.

Jane Brown and her colleagues concluded from their years of research that the mass media are important sex educators for American teenagers. Other potential educators, such as parents, schools, and churches, are doing an inadequate job, and even if that were to change dramatically, the media would remain compelling teachers. Brown faults media portrayals for avoiding the "three C's"—commitment, contraceptives, and consequences—and concludes, "It is little wonder that adolescents find the sexual world a difficult and often confusing place and that they engage in early and unprotected sexual intercourse with multiple partners."

The emphasis for girls and women is always on being desirable, not on experiencing desire. Girls who want to be sexually *active* instead of simply being the objects of male desire are given only one model to follow, that of exploitive male sexuality. It seems that advertisers can't conceive of a kind of power that isn't manipulative and exploitive or a way that women can be actively sexual without being like traditional men.

Women who are "powerful" in advertising are uncommitted. They treat men like sex objects: "If I want a man to see my bra, I take him home," says an androgynous young woman. They are elusive and distant: "She is the first woman who refused to take your phone calls," says one ad. As if it were a good thing to be rude and inconsiderate. Why should any of us, male or female, be interested in someone who won't take our phone calls, who either cares so little for us or is so manipulative?

Mostly though, girls are not supposed to have sexual agency. They are supposed to be passive, swept away, overpowered. "See where it takes you," says a perfume ad featuring a couple passionately embracing. "Unleash your fantasies," says another. "A force of nature." This contributes to the strange and damaging concept of the "good girl" as the one who is swept away, unprepared for sex, versus the "bad girl" as the one who plans for sex, uses contraception, and is generally responsible. A young woman can manage to have sex and yet in some sense maintain her virginity by being "out of control," drunk, or deep in denial about the entire experience.

No wonder most teenage pregnancies occur when one or both parties is drunk. Alcohol and other mind-altering drugs permit sexual activity at the same time that they allow denial. One is almost literally not there. The next day one has an excuse. I was drunk, I was swept away. I did not choose this experience.

In adolescence girls are told that they have to give up much of what they *know* about relationships and intimacy if they want to attract men. Most tragically, they are told they have to give up each other. The truth is that one of the most powerful antidotes to destructive cultural messages is close and supportive female friendships. But girls are often encouraged by the culture to sacrifice their relationships with each other and to enter into hostile competition for the attention of boys and men. "What the bitch who's about to steal your man wears," says one ad. And many ads feature young women fighting or glaring at each other.

Of course, some girls do resist and rebel. Some are encouraged (by someone—a loving parent, a supportive teacher) to see the cultural contradictions clearly and to break free in a healthy and positive way. Others rebel in ways that damage themselves. A young woman seems to have only two choices: She can bury her sexual self, be a "good girl," give in to what Carol Gilligan terms "the tyranny of nice and kind" (and numb the pain by overeating or starving or cutting herself or drinking heavily). Or she can become a rebel—flaunt her sexuality, seduce inappropriate partners, smoke, drink flamboyantly, use other drugs. Both of these responses are self-destructive, but they begin as an attempt to survive, not to self-destruct.

* * *

STUDY QUESTIONS

1. Why does Kilbourne believe the constant barrage of ads telling women they must be thin to have any value is "cutting them down to size"?

2. Kilbourne argues that women are presented with conflicting images of the "ideal woman." Give a few examples of these conflicting messages.

3. When you ask a room full of students, "Are people affected by advertising and the media?" almost everyone says, "Of course." However, if you ask individual students, "Is how you see the world affected by advertising and the media?" almost everyone says no. How is it possible that "people" have this problem, but almost no individual does? What does this tell us about why people do not react more strongly when they see ads and **media** like the ones Kilbourne discusses in her article?

4. This article was written in 1999. Maybe advertising and the media have changed how they present men and women. Look online, through magazines, or any other form of media and find five ads or images that either support or challenge the arguments Kilbourne makes about how women and girls are shown. Print/copy your advertisements and/or media and bring them to discuss in class.

BARBARA EHRENREICH

Nickel and Dimed: On (Not) Getting By in America

After hurricane Katrina, most Americans were shocked to see the poverty and isolation of communities affected by the disaster. Indeed, Katrina uncovered the pervasive **social inequality** in American life. In this article Barbara Ehrenreich similarly unveils the plight of the **working poor** and the conditions they must endure to make ends meet, through an **ethnographic** experiment. She asks us to look beyond our individualistic realities to observe the recurrent inequalities plaguing our social landscape. Too often we overlook or deny such inequities.

AT THE BEGINNING OF JUNE 1998 I LEAVE BEHIND EVERYTHING THAT normally soothes the ego and sustains the body—home, career, companion, reputation, ATM card—for a plunge into the low-wage workforce. There, I become another, occupationally much diminished "Barbara Ehrenreich"—depicted on job-application forms as a divorced homemaker whose sole work experience consists of housekeeping in a few private homes. I am terrified, at the beginning, of being unmasked for what I am: a middle-class journalist setting out to explore the world that welfare mothers are entering, at the rate of approximately 50,000 a month, as welfare reform[1] kicks in. Happily, though, my fears turn out to be entirely unwarranted: during a month of poverty and toil, my name goes unnoticed and for the most part unuttered. In this parallel

---

[1] In 1996, the U.S. Congress passed the Personal Responsibility and Work Opportunity Reconciliation Act, which established time limits on federal assistance for the poor and required that those seeking assistance work or train for work. [Ed. Unless otherwise indicated, as here, footnotes are those of the author.]

universe where my father never got out of the mines and I never got through college, I am "baby," "honey," "blondie," and, most commonly, "girl."

My first task is to find a place to live. I figure that if I can earn $7 an hour—which, from the want ads, seems doable—I can afford to spend $500 on rent, or maybe, with severe economies, $600. In the Key West area, where I live, this pretty much confines me to flophouses and trailer homes—like the one, a pleasing fifteen-minute drive from town, that has no air-conditioning, no screens, no fans, no television, and, by way of diversion, only the challenge of evading the landlord's Doberman pinscher. The big problem with this place, though, is the rent, which at $675 a month is well beyond my reach. All right, Key West is expensive. But so is New York City, or the Bay Area, or Jackson Hole, or Telluride, or Boston, or any other place where tourists and the wealthy compete for living space with the people who clean their toilets and fry their hash browns.[2] Still, it is a shock to realize that "trailer trash" has become, for me, a demographic category to aspire to.

So I decide to make the common trade-off between affordability and convenience, and go for a $500-a-month efficiency thirty miles up a two-lane highway from the employment opportunities of Key West, meaning forty-five minutes if there's no road construction and I don't get caught behind some sun-dazed Canadian tourists. I hate the drive, along a roadside studded with white crosses commemorating the more effective head-on collisions, but it's a sweet little place—a cabin, more or less, set in the swampy backyard of the converted mobile home where my landlord, an affable TV repairman, lives with his bartender girlfriend. Anthropologically speaking, a bustling trailer park would be preferable, but here I have a gleaming white floor and a firm mattress, and the few resident bugs are easily vanquished.

Besides, I am not doing this for the anthropology. My aim is nothing so mistily subjective as to "experience poverty" or find out how it "really feels" to be a long-term low-wage worker. I've had enough unchosen encounters with poverty and the world of low-wage work to know it's not a place you want to visit for touristic purposes; it just smells too much like fear. And with all my real-life assets—bank account, IRA, health insurance, multiroom home—waiting indulgently in the background, I am, of course, thoroughly insulated from the terrors that afflict the genuinely poor.

No, this is a purely objective, scientific sort of mission. The humanitarian rationale for welfare reform—as opposed to the more punitive and stingy impulses that may actually have motivated it—is that work will lift poor women out of poverty while simultaneously inflating their self-esteem and hence their future value in the labor market. Thus, whatever the hassles involved in finding child care, transportation, etc.,

---

[2] According to the Department of Housing and Urban Development, the "fair-market rent" for an efficiency is $551 here in Monroe County, Florida. A comparable rent in the five boroughs of New York City is $704; in San Francisco, $713; and in the heart of Silicon Valley, $808. The fair-market rent for an area is defined as the amount that would be needed to pay rent plus utilities for "privately owned, decent, safe, and sanitary rental housing of a modest (non-luxury) nature with suitable amenities."

the transition from welfare to work will end happily, in greater prosperity for all. Now there are many problems with this comforting prediction, such as the fact that the economy will inevitably undergo a downturn, eliminating many jobs. Even without a downturn, the influx of a million former welfare recipients into the low-wage labor market could depress wages by as much as 11.9 percent, according to the Economic Policy Institute (EPI) in Washington, D.C.

But is it really possible to make a living on the kinds of jobs currently available to unskilled people? Mathematically, the answer is no, as can be shown by taking $6 to $7 an hour, perhaps subtracting a dollar or two an hour for child care, multiplying by 160 hours a month, and comparing the result to the prevailing rents. According to the National Coalition for the Homeless, for example, in 1998 it took, on average nationwide, an hourly wage of $8.89 to afford a one-bedroom apartment, and the Preamble Center for Public Policy estimates that the odds against a typical welfare recipient's landing a job at such a "living wage" are about 97 to 1. If these numbers are right, low-wage work is not a solution to poverty and possibly not even to homelessness.

It may seem excessive to put this proposition to an experimental test. As certain family members keep unhelpfully reminding me, the viability of low-wage work could be tested, after a fashion, without ever leaving my study. I could just pay myself $7 an hour for eight hours a day, charge myself for room and board, and total up the numbers after a month. Why leave the people and work that I love? But I am an experimental scientist by training. In that business, you don't just sit at a desk and theorize; you plunge into the everyday chaos of nature, where surprises lurk in the most mundane measurements. Maybe, when I got into it, I would discover some hidden economies in the world of the low-wage worker. After all, if 30 percent of the workforce toils for less than $8 an hour, according to the EPI, they may have found some tricks as yet unknown to me. Maybe—who knows?—I would even be able to detect in myself the bracing psychological effects of getting out of the house, as promised by the welfare wonks at places like the Heritage Foundation. Or, on the other hand, maybe there would be unexpected costs—physical, mental, or financial—to throw off all my calculations. Ideally, I should do this with two small children in tow, that being the welfare average, but mine are grown and no one is willing to lend me theirs for a month-long vacation in penury. So this is not the perfect experiment, just a test of the best possible case: an unencumbered woman, smart and even strong, attempting to live more or less off the land.

On the morning of my first full day of job searching, I take a red pen to the want ads, which are suspiciously numerous. Everyone in Key West's booming "hospitality industry" seems to be looking for someone like me—trainable, flexible, and with suitably humble expectations as to pay. I know I possess certain traits that might be advantageous—I'm white and, I like to think, well-spoken and poised—but I decide on two rules: One, I cannot use any skills derived from my education or usual work—not that there are a lot of want ads for satirical essayists anyway. Two, I have to take the best-paid job that is offered me and of course do my best to hold it[.] * * * In addition, I rule out various occupations for one reason or another: Hotel front-desk clerk, for example, which to my surprise is regarded as unskilled and pays around $7 an hour, gets eliminated because it involves standing in one spot for eight hours a day. Waitressing is similarly something I'd like to avoid, because I remember it leaving me bone tired when I was eighteen, and I'm decades of varicosities and back pain beyond that now. Telemarketing, one of the first refuges of the suddenly indigent, can be dismissed on grounds of personality. This leaves certain supermarket jobs, such as deli clerk, or housekeeping in Key West's thousands of hotel and guest rooms. Housekeeping is especially appealing, for reasons both atavistic and practical: it's what my mother did before I came along, and it can't be too different from what I've been doing part-time, in my own home, all my life.

So I put on what I take to be a respectful-looking outfit of ironed Bermuda shorts and scooped-neck T-shirt and set out for a tour of the local hotels and supermarkets. Best Western, Econo Lodge, and HoJo's all let me fill out application forms, and these are, to my relief, interested in little more than whether I am a legal resident of the United States and have committed any felonies. My next stop is Winn-Dixie, the supermarket, which turns out to have a particularly onerous application process, featuring a fifteen-minute "interview" by computer since, apparently, no human on the premises is deemed capable of representing the corporate point of view. I am conducted to a large room decorated with posters illustrating how to look "professional" (it helps to be white and, if female, permed) and warning of the slick promises that union organizers might try to tempt me with. The interview is multiple choice: Do I have anything, such as child-care problems, that might make it hard for me to get to work on time? Do I think safety on the job is the responsibility of management? Then, popping up cunningly out of the blue: How many dollars' worth of stolen goods have I purchased in the last year? Would I turn in a fellow employee if I caught him stealing? Finally, "Are you an honest person?"

Apparently, I ace the interview, because I am told that all I have to do is show up in some doctor's office tomorrow for a urine test. This seems to be a fairly general rule: if you want to stack Cheerio boxes or vacuum hotel rooms in chemically fascist America, you have to be willing to squat down and pee in front of some health worker (who has no doubt had to do the same thing herself). The wages Winn-Dixie is offering—$6 and a couple of dimes to start with—are not enough, I decide, to compensate for this indignity.[3]

I lunch at Wendy's, where $4.99 gets you unlimited refills at the Mexican part of the Superbar, a comforting surfeit of refried beans and "cheese sauce." A teenage

---

[3] According to the *Monthly Labor Review* (November 1996), 28 percent of work sites surveyed in the service industry conduct drug tests (corporate workplaces have much higher rates), and the incidence of testing has risen markedly since the Eighties. The rate of testing is highest in the South (56 percent of work sites polled), with the Midwest in second place (50 percent). The drug most likely to be detected—marijuana, which can be detected in urine for weeks—is also the most innocuous, while heroin and cocaine are generally undetectable three days after use.

employee, seeing me studying the want ads, kindly offers me an application form, which I fill out, though here, too, the pay is just $6 and change an hour. Then it's off for a round of the locally owned inns and guesthouses. At "The Palms," let's call it, a bouncy manager actually takes me around to see the rooms and meet the existing housekeepers, who, I note with satisfaction, look pretty much like me—faded ex-hippie types in shorts with long hair pulled back in braids. Mostly, though, no one speaks to me or even looks at me except to proffer an application form. At my last stop, a palatial B&B, I wait twenty minutes to meet "Max," only to be told that there are no jobs now but there should be one soon, since "nobody lasts more than a couple weeks." (Because none of the people I talked to knew I was a reporter, I have changed their names to protect their privacy and, in some cases perhaps, their jobs.)

Three days go by like this, and, to my chagrin, no one out of the approximately twenty places I've applied calls me for an interview. I had been vain enough to worry about coming across as too educated for the jobs I sought, but no one even seems interested in finding out how overqualified I am. Only later will I realize that the want ads are not a reliable measure of the actual jobs available at any particular time. They are, as I should have guessed from Max's comment, the employers' insurance policy against the relentless turnover of the low-wage work force. Most of the big hotels run ads almost continually, just to build a supply of applicants to replace the current workers as they drift away or are fired, so finding a job is just a matter of being at the right place at the right time and flexible enough to take whatever is being offered that day. This finally happens to me at one of the big discount hotel chains, where I go, as usual, for housekeeping and am sent, instead, to try out as a waitress at the attached "family restaurant," a dismal spot with a counter and about thirty tables that looks out on a parking garage and features such tempting fare as "Pollish [*sic*] sausage and BBQ sauce" on 95-degree days. Phillip, the dapper young West Indian who introduces himself as the manager, interviews me with about as much enthusiasm as if he were a clerk processing me for Medicare, the principal questions being what shifts can I work and when can I start. I mutter something about being woefully out of practice as a waitress, but he's already on to the uniform: I'm to show up tomorrow wearing black slacks and black shoes; he'll provide the rust-colored polo shirt with hearthside embroidered on it, though I might want to wear my own shirt to get to work, ha ha. At the word "tomorrow," something between fear and indignation rises in my chest. I want to say, "Thank you for your time, sir, but this is just an experiment, you know, not my actual life."

So begins my career at the Hearthside, I shall call it, one small profit center within a global discount hotel chain, where for two weeks I work from 2:00 till 10:00 p.m. for $2.43 an hour plus tips.[4] In some futile bid for gentility, the management has barred

---

[4] According to the Fair Labor Standards Act, employers are not required to pay "tipped employees," such as restaurant servers, more than $2.13 an hour in direct wages. However, if the sum of tips

employees from using the front door, so my first day I enter through the kitchen, where a red-faced man with shoulder-length blond hair is throwing frozen steaks against the wall and yelling, "Fuck this shit!" "That's just Jack," explains Gail, the wiry middle-aged waitress who is assigned to train me. "He's on the rag again"—a condition occasioned, in this instance, by the fact that the cook on the morning shift had forgotten to thaw out the steaks. For the next eight hours, I run after the agile Gail, absorbing bits of instruction along with fragments of personal tragedy. All food must be trayed, and the reason she's so tired today is that she woke up in a cold sweat thinking of her boyfriend, who killed himself recently in an upstate prison. No refills on lemonade. And the reason he was in prison is that a few DUIs caught up with him, that's all, could have happened to anyone. Carry the creamers to the table in a monkey bowl, never in your hand. And after he was gone she spent several months living in her truck, peeing in a plastic pee bottle and reading by candlelight at night, but you can't live in a truck in the summer, since you need to have the windows down, which means anything can get in, from mosquitoes on up.

At least Gail puts to rest any fears I had of appearing overqualified. From the first day on, I find that of all the things I have left behind, such as home and identity, what I miss the most is competence. Not that I have ever felt utterly competent in the writing business, in which one day's success augurs nothing at all for the next. But in my writing life, I at least have some notion of procedure: do the research, make the outline, rough out a draft, etc. As a server, though, I am beset by requests like bees: more iced tea here, ketchup over there, a to-go box for table fourteen, and where are the high chairs, anyway? Of the twenty-seven tables, up to six are usually mine at any time, though on slow afternoons or if Gail is off, I sometimes have the whole place to myself. There is the touch-screen computer-ordering system to master, which is, I suppose, meant to minimize server-cook contact, but in practice requires constant verbal fine-tuning: "That's gravy on the mashed, okay? None on the meatloaf," and so forth—while the cook scowls as if I were inventing these refinements just to torment him. Plus, something I had forgotten in the years since I was eighteen: about a third of a server's job is "side work" that's invisible to customers—sweeping, scrubbing, slicing, refilling, and restocking. If it isn't all done, every little bit of it, you're going to face the 6:00 P.M. dinner rush defenseless and probably go down in flames. I screw up dozens of times at the beginning, sustained in my shame entirely by Gail's support—"It's okay, baby, everyone does that sometime"—because, to my total surprise and despite the scientific detachment I am doing my best to maintain, I care.

The whole thing would be a lot easier if I could just skate through it as Lily Tomlin in one of her waitress skits, but I was raised by the absurd Booker T. Washingtonian

---

plus $2.13 an hour falls below the minimum wage, or $5.15 an hour, the employer is required to make up the difference. This fact was not mentioned by managers or otherwise publicized at either of the restaurants where I worked.

precept that says: If you're going to do something, do it well. In fact, "well" isn't good enough by half. Do it better than anyone has ever done it before. Or so said my father, who must have known what he was talking about because he managed to pull himself, and us with him, up from the mile-deep copper mines of Butte to the leafy suburbs of the Northeast, ascending from boilermakers to martinis before booze beat out ambition. As in most endeavors I have encountered in my life, doing it "better than anyone" is not a reasonable goal. Still, when I wake up at 4:00 A.M. in my own cold sweat, I am not thinking about the writing deadlines I'm neglecting; I'm thinking about the table whose order I screwed up so that one of the boys didn't get his kiddie meal until the rest of the family had moved on to their Key Lime pies. That's the other powerful motivation I hadn't expected—the customers, or "patients," as I can't help thinking of them on account of the mysterious vulnerability that seems to have left them temporarily unable to feed themselves. After a few days at the Hearthside, I feel the service ethic kick in like a shot of oxytocin, the nurturance hormone. The plurality of my customers are hardworking locals—truck drivers, construction workers, even housekeepers from the attached hotel—and I want them to have the closest to a "fine dining" experience that the grubby circumstances will allow. No "you guys" for me; everyone over twelve is "sir" or "ma'am." I ply them with iced tea and coffee refills; I return, mid-meal, to inquire how everything is; I doll up their salads with chopped raw mushrooms, summer squash slices, or whatever bits of produce I can find that have survived their sojourn in the cold-storage room mold-free.

* * *

Ten days into it, this is beginning to look like a livable lifestyle. I like Gail, who is "looking at fifty" but moves so fast she can alight in one place and then another without apparently being anywhere between them. I clown around with Lionel, the teenage Haitian busboy, and catch a few fragments of conversation with Joan, the svelte fortyish hostess and militant feminist who is the only one of us who dares to tell Jack to shut the fuck up. I even warm up to Jack when, on a slow night and to make up for a particularly unwarranted attack on my abilities, or so I imagine, he tells me about his glory days as a young man at "coronary school"—or do you say "culinary"?—in Brooklyn, where he dated a knock-out Puerto Rican chick and learned everything there is to know about food. I finish up at 10:00 or 10:30, depending on how much side work I've been able to get done during the shift, and cruise home[.] * * * To bed by 1:30 or 2:00, up at 9:00 or 10:00, read for an hour while my uniform whirls around in the landlord's washing machine, and then it's another eight hours spent following Mao's central instruction, as laid out in the Little Red Book, which was: Serve the people.

I could drift along like this, in some dreamy proletarian idyll, except for two things. One is management. If I have kept this subject on the margins thus far it is because I still flinch to think that I spent all those weeks under the surveillance of men (and later women) whose job it was to monitor my behavior for signs of sloth, theft, drug abuse, or worse. Not that managers and especially "assistant managers" in low-wage settings like this are exactly the class enemy. In the restaurant business, they are mostly former cooks or servers, still capable of pinch-hitting in the kitchen or on the floor, just as in hotels they are likely to be former clerks, and paid a salary of only about $400 a week. But everyone knows they have crossed over to the other side, which is, crudely put, corporate as opposed to human. Cooks want to prepare tasty meals; servers want to serve them graciously; but managers are there for only one reason—to make sure that money is made for some theoretical entity that exists far away in Chicago or New York, if a corporation can be said to have a physical existence at all. Reflecting on her career, Gail tells me ruefully that she had sworn, years ago, never to work for a corporation again. "They don't cut you no slack. You give and you give, and they take."

Managers can sit—for hours at a time if they want—but it's their job to see that no one else ever does, even when there's nothing to do, and this is why, for servers, slow times can be as exhausting as rushes. You start dragging out each little chore, because if the manager on duty catches you in an idle moment, he will give you something far nastier to do. So I wipe, I clean, I consolidate ketchup bottles and recheck the cheesecake supply, even tour the tables to make sure the customer evaluation forms are all standing perkily in their places—wondering all the time how many calories I burn in these strictly theatrical exercises. When, on a particularly dead afternoon, Stu finds me glancing at a *USA Today* a customer has left behind, he assigns me to vacuum the entire floor with the broken vacuum cleaner that has a handle only two feet long, and the only way to do that without incurring orthopedic damage is to proceed from spot to spot on your knees.

On my first Friday at the Hearthside there is a "mandatory meeting for all restaurant employees," which I attend, eager for insight into our overall marketing strategy and the niche (your basic Ohio cuisine with a tropical twist?) we aim to inhabit. But there is no "we" at this meeting. Phillip, our top manager except for an occasional "consultant" sent out by corporate headquarters, opens it with a sneer: "The break room—it's disgusting. Butts in the ashtrays, newspapers lying around, crumbs." This windowless little room, which also houses the time clock for the entire hotel, is where we stash our bags and civilian clothes and take our half-hour meal breaks. But a break room is not a right, he tells us. It can be taken away. We should also know that the lockers in the break room and whatever is in them can be searched at any time. Then comes gossip; there has been gossip; gossip (which seems to mean employees talking among themselves) must stop. Off-duty employees are henceforth barred from eating at the restaurant, because "other servers gather around them and gossip." When Phillip has exhausted his agenda of rebukes, Joan complains about the condition of the ladies' room and I throw in my two bits about the vacuum cleaner. But I don't see any backup coming from my fellow servers, each of whom has subsided into her own personal funk; Gail, my role model, stares sorrowfully at a point six inches from her nose.

The meeting ends when Andy, one of the cooks, gets up, muttering about breaking up his day off for this almighty bullshit.

Just four days later we are suddenly summoned into the kitchen at 3:30 P.M., even though there are live tables on the floor. We all—about ten of us—stand around Phillip, who announces grimly that there has been a report of some "drug activity" on the night shift and that, as a result, we are now to be a "drug-free" workplace, meaning that all new hires will be tested, as will possibly current employees on a random basis. I am glad that this part of the kitchen is so dark, because I find myself blushing as hard as if I had been caught toking up in the ladies' room myself: I haven't been treated this way—lined up in the corridor, threatened with locker searches, peppered with carelessly aimed accusations—since junior high school.

*   *   *

The other problem, in addition to the less-than-nurturing management style, is that this job shows no sign of being financially viable. You might imagine, from a comfortable distance, that people who live, year in and year out, on $6 to $10 an hour have discovered some survival stratagems unknown to the middle class. But no. It's not hard to get my co-workers to talk about their living situations, because housing, in almost every case, is the principal source of disruption in their lives, the first thing they fill you in on when they arrive for their shifts. After a week, I have compiled the following survey:

- Gail is sharing a room in a well-known downtown flophouse for which she and a roommate pay about $250 a week. Her roommate, a male friend, has begun hitting on her, driving her nuts, but the rent would be impossible alone.
- Claude, the Haitian cook, is desperate to get out of the two-room apartment he shares with his girlfriend and two other, unrelated, people. As far as I can determine, the other Haitian men (most of whom only speak Creole) live in similarly crowded situations.
- Annette, a twenty-year-old server who is six months pregnant and has been abandoned by her boyfriend, lives with her mother, a postal clerk.
- Marianne and her boyfriend are paying $170 a week for a one-person trailer.
- Jack, who is, at $10 an hour, the wealthiest of us, lives in the trailer he owns, paying only the $400-a-month lot fee.
- The other white cook, Andy, lives on his dry-docked boat, which, as far as I can tell from his loving descriptions, can't be more than twenty feet long. He offers to take me out on it, once it's repaired, but the offer comes with inquiries as to my marital status, so I do not follow up on it.
- Tina and her husband are paying $60 a night for a double room in a Days Inn. This is because they have no car and the Days Inn is within walking distance of the Hearthside. When Marianne, one of the breakfast servers, is tossed out of her

trailer for subletting (which is against the trailer-park rules), she leaves her boy-friend and moves in with Tina and her husband.

- Joan, who had fooled me with her numerous and tasteful outfits (hostesses wear their own clothes), lives in a van she parks behind a shopping center at night and showers in Tina's motel room. The clothes are from thrift shops.[5]

It strikes me, in my middle-class solipsism, that there is gross improvidence in some of these arrangements. When Gail and I are wrapping silverware in napkins—the only task for which we are permitted to sit—she tells me she is thinking of escaping from her roommate by moving into the Days Inn herself. I am astounded: How can she even think of paying between $40 and $60 a day? But if I was afraid of sounding like a social worker, I come out just sounding like a fool. She squints at me in disbelief, "And where am I supposed to get a month's rent and a month's deposit for an apartment?" I'd been feeling pretty smug about my $500 efficiency, but of course it was made possible only by the $1,300 I had allotted myself for start-up costs when I began my low-wage life: $1,000 for the first month's rent and deposit, $100 for initial groceries and cash in my pocket, $200 stuffed away for emergencies. In poverty, as in certain propositions in physics, starting conditions are everything.

There are no secret economies that nourish the poor; on the contrary, there are a host of special costs. If you can't put up the two months' rent you need to secure an apartment, you end up paying through the nose for a room by the week. If you have only a room, with a hot plate at best, you can't save by cooking up huge lentil stews that can be frozen for the week ahead. You eat fast food, or the hot dogs and styrofoam cups of soup that can be microwaved in a convenience store. If you have no money for health insurance—and the Hearthside's niggardly plan kicks in only after three months—you go without routine care or prescription drugs and end up paying the price.

* * *

My own situation, when I sit down to assess it after two weeks of work, would not be much better if this were my actual life. The seductive thing about waitressing is that you don't have to wait for payday to feel a few bills in your pocket, and my tips usu-ally cover meals and gas, plus something left over to stuff into the kitchen drawer I use as a bank. But as the tourist business slows in the summer heat, I sometimes leave work with only $20 in tips (the gross is higher, but servers share about 15 percent of their tips with the busboys and bartenders). With wages included, this amounts to about the minimum wage of $5.15 an hour. Although the sum in the drawer is piling up, at the present rate of accumulation it will be more than a hundred dollars short of my

---

[5] I could find no statistics on the number of employed people living in cars or vans, but according to the National Coalition for the Homeless's 1997 report "Myths and Facts About Homelessness," nearly one in five homeless people (in twenty-nine cities across the nation) is employed in a full- or part-time job.

rent when the end of the month comes around. Nor can I see any expenses to cut. True, I haven't gone the lentil-stew route yet, but that's because I don't have a large cooking pot, pot holders, or a ladle to stir with (which cost about $30 at Kmart, less at thrift stores), not to mention onions, carrots, and the indispensable bay leaf. I do make my lunch almost every day—usually some slow-burning, high-protein combo like frozen chicken patties with melted cheese on top and canned pinto beans on the side. Dinner is at the Hearthside, which offers its employees a choice of BLT, fish sandwich, or hamburger for only $2. The burger lasts longest, especially if it's heaped with gut-puckering jalapeños, but by midnight my stomach is growling again.

So unless I want to start using my car as a residence, I have to find a second, or alternative, job. I call all the hotels where I filled out housekeeping applications weeks ago—the Hyatt, Holiday Inn, Econo Lodge, HoJo's, Best Western, plus a half dozen or so locally run guesthouses. Nothing. Then I start making the rounds again, wasting whole mornings waiting for some assistant manager to show up, even dipping into places so creepy that the front-desk clerk greets you from behind bulletproof glass and sells pints of liquor over the counter. But either someone has exposed my real-life housekeeping habits—which are, shall we say, mellow—or I am at the wrong end of some infallible ethnic equation: most, but by no means all, of the working housekeepers I see on my job searches are African Americans, Spanish-speaking, or immigrants from the Central European post-Communist world, whereas servers are almost invariably white and monolingually English-speaking. When I finally get a positive response, I have been identified once again as server material. Jerry's, which is part of a well-known national family restaurant chain and physically attached here to another budget hotel chain, is ready to use me at once. The prospect is both exciting and terrifying, because, with about the same number of tables and counter seats, Jerry's attracts three or four times the volume of customers as the gloomy old Hearthside.

Picture a fat person's hell, and I don't mean a place with no food. Instead there is everything you might eat if eating had no bodily consequences—cheese fries, chicken-fried steaks, fudge-laden desserts—only here every bite must be paid for, one way or another, in human discomfort. The kitchen is a cavern, a stomach leading to the lower intestine that is the garbage and dish-washing area, from which issue bizarre smells combining the edible and the offal: creamy carrion, pizza barf, and that unique and enigmatic Jerry's scent—citrus fart. The floor is slick with spills, forcing us to walk through the kitchen with tiny steps[.] * * * Sinks everywhere are clogged with scraps of lettuce, decomposing lemon wedges, waterlogged toast crusts. Put your hand down on any counter and you risk being stuck to it by the film of ancient syrup spills, and this is unfortunate, because hands are utensils here, used for scooping up lettuce onto salad plates, lifting out pie slices, and even moving hash browns from one plate to another. The regulation poster in the single unisex restroom admonishes us to wash our hands thoroughly and even offers instructions for doing so, but there is always some vital substance missing—soap, paper towels, toilet paper—and I never find all three at once. You learn to stuff your pockets with napkins before going in there, and too bad about the customers, who must eat, though they don't realize this, almost literally out of our hands.

The break room typifies the whole situation: there is none, because there are no breaks at Jerry's. For six to eight hours in a row, you never sit except to pee. Actually, there are three folding chairs at a table immediately adjacent to the bathroom, but hardly anyone ever sits here, in the very rectum of the gastro-architectural system. Rather, the function of the peritoilet area is to house the ashtrays in which servers and dishwashers leave their cigarettes burning at all times, like votive candles, so that they don't have to waste time lighting up again when they dash back for a puff. Almost everyone smokes as if his or her pulmonary well-being depended on it—the multinational mélange of cooks, the Czech dishwashers, the servers, who are all American natives—creating an atmosphere in which oxygen is only an occasional pollutant. My first morning at Jerry's, when the hypoglycemic shakes set in, I complain to one of my fellow servers that I don't understand how she can go so long without food. "Well, I don't understand how you can go so long without a cigarette," she responds in a tone of reproach—because work is what you do for others; smoking is what you do for yourself. I don't know why the anti-smoking crusaders have never grasped the element of defiant self-nurturance that makes the habit so endearing to its victims—as if, in the American workplace, the only thing people have to call their own is the tumors they are nourishing and the spare moments they devote to feeding them.

Now, the Industrial Revolution is not an easy transition, especially when you have to zip through it in just a couple of days. I have gone from craft work straight into the factory, from the air-conditioned morgue of the Hearth-side directly into the flames. Customers arrive in human waves, sometimes disgorged fifty at a time from their tour buses, peckish and whiny. Instead of two "girls" on the floor at once, there can be as many as six of us running around in our brilliant pink-and-orange Hawaiian shirts.

* * *

I start out with the beautiful, heroic idea of handling the two jobs at once, and for two days I almost do it: the breakfast/lunch shift at Jerry's, which goes till 2:00, arriving at the Hearthside at 2:10, and attempting to hold out until 10:00. In the ten minutes between jobs, I pick up a spicy chicken sandwich at the Wendy's drive-through window, gobble it down in the car, and change from khaki slacks to black, from Hawaiian to rust polo. There is a problem, though. When during the 3:00 to 4:00 P.M. dead time I finally sit down to wrap silver, my flesh seems to bond to the seat. I try to refuel with a purloined cup of soup, as I've seen Gail and Joan do dozens of times, but a manager catches me and hisses "No eating!" though there's not a customer around to be offended by the sight of food making contact with a server's lips. So I tell Gail I'm going to quit, and she hugs me and says she might just follow me to Jerry's herself.

But the chances of this are minuscule. She has left the flophouse and her annoying roommate and is back to living in her beat-up old truck. But guess what? she reports to me excitedly later that evening: Phillip has given her permission to park overnight in the hotel parking lot, as long as she keeps out of sight, and the parking lot should be totally safe, since it's patrolled by a hotel security guard! With the Hearthside offering benefits like that, how could anyone think of leaving?

Gail would have triumphed at Jerry's, I'm sure, but for me it's a crash course in exhaustion management. Years ago, the kindly fry cook who trained me to waitress at a Los Angeles truck stop used to say: Never make an unnecessary trip; if you don't have to walk fast, walk slow; if you don't have to walk, stand. But at Jerry's the effort of distinguishing necessary from unnecessary and urgent from whenever would itself be too much of an energy drain. The only thing to do is to treat each shift as a one-time-only emergency; you've got fifty starving people out there, lying scattered on the battlefield, so get out there and feed them! Forget that you will have to do this again tomorrow, forget that you will have to be alert enough to dodge the drunks on the drive home tonight—just burn, burn, burn! Ideally, at some point you enter what servers call "a rhythm" and psychologists term a "flow state," in which signals pass from the sense organs directly to the muscles, bypassing the cerebral cortex, and a Zen-like emptiness sets in. * * *

But there's another capacity of the neuromuscular system, which is pain. I start tossing back drugstore-brand ibuprofen pills as if they were vitamin C, four before each shift, because an old mouse-related repetitive-stress injury in my upper back has come back to full-spasm strength, thanks to the tray carrying. In my ordinary life, this level of disability might justify a day of ice packs and stretching.

* * *

I make friends, over time, with the other "girls" who work my shift: Nita, the tattooed twenty-something who taunts us by going around saying brightly, "Have we started making money yet?" Ellen, whose teenage son cooks on the graveyard shift and who once managed a restaurant in Massachusetts but won't try out for management here because she prefers being a "common worker" and not "ordering people around." Easy-going fiftyish Lucy, with the raucous laugh, who limps toward the end of the shift because of something that has gone wrong with her leg, the exact nature of which cannot be determined without health insurance. We talk about the usual girl things—men, children, and the sinister allure of Jerry's chocolate peanut-butter cream pie—though no one, I notice, ever brings up anything potentially expensive, like shopping or movies. As at the Hearthside, the only recreation ever referred to is partying, which requires little more than some beer, a joint, and a few close friends. Still, no one here is homeless, or cops to it anyway, thanks usually to a working husband or boyfriend. All in all, we form a reliable mutual-support group: If one of us is feeling sick or overwhelmed, another one will "bev" a table or even carry trays for her. If one of us is off sneaking a cigarette or a pee,[6] the others will do their best to conceal her absence from the enforcers of corporate rationality.

But my saving human connection—my oxytocin receptor, as it were—is George, the nineteen-year-old, fresh-off-the-boat Czech dishwasher. We get to talking when he asks me, tortuously, how much cigarettes cost at Jerry's. I do my best to explain that they cost over a dollar more here than at a regular store and suggest that he just take one from the half-filled packs that are always lying around on the break table. But that would be unthinkable. Except for the one tiny earring signaling his allegiance to some vaguely alternative point of view, George is a perfect straight arrow—crew-cut, hard-working, and hungry for eye contact. "Czech Republic," I ask, "or Slovakia?" and he seems delighted that I know the difference. "Václav Havel," I try. "Velvet Revolution, Frank Zappa!" "Yes, yes, 1989," he says, and I realize we are talking about history.

* * *

I make the decision to move closer to Key West. First, because of the drive. Second and third, also because of the drive: gas is eating up $4 to $5 a day, and although Jerry's is as high-volume as you can get, the tips average only 10 percent, and not just for a newbie like me. Between the base pay of $2.15 an hour and the obligation to share tips with the busboys and dishwashers, we're averaging only about $7.50 an hour. Then there is the $30 I had to spend on the regulation tan slacks worn by Jerry's servers—a setback it could take weeks to absorb. (I had combed the town's two down-scale department stores hoping for something cheaper but decided in the end that these marked-down Dockers, originally $49, were more likely to survive a daily washing.) Of my fellow servers, everyone who lacks a working husband or boyfriend seems to have a second job: Nita does something at a computer eight hours a day; another welds. Without the forty-five-minute commute, I can picture myself working two jobs and having the time to shower between them.

So I take the $500 deposit I have coming from my landlord, the $400 I have earned toward the next month's rent, plus the $200 reserved for emergencies, and use the $1,100 to pay the rent and deposit on trailer number 46 in the Overseas Trailer Park, a

---

[6] Until April 1998, there was no federally mandated right to bathroom breaks. According to Marc Linder and Ingrid Nygaard, authors of *Void Where Prohibited: Rest Breaks and the Right to Urinate on Company Time* (Cornell University Press, 1997), "The right to rest and void at work is not high on the list of social or political causes supported by professional or executive employees, who enjoy personal workplace liberties that millions of factory workers can only daydream about.... While we were dismayed to discover that workers lacked an acknowledged legal right to void at work, [the workers] were amazed by outsiders' naive belief that their employers would permit them to perform this basic bodily function when necessary.... A factory worker, not allowed a break for six-hour stretches, voided into pads worn inside her uniform; and a kindergarten teacher in a school without aides had to take all twenty children with her to the bathroom and line them up outside the stall door when she voided."

mile from the cluster of budget hotels that constitute Key West's version of an industrial park. Number 46 is about eight feet in width and shaped like a barbell inside, with a narrow region—because of the sink and the stove—separating the bedroom from what might optimistically be called the "living" area, with its two-person table and half-sized couch. The bathroom is so small my knees rub against the shower stall when I sit on the toilet, and you can't just leap out of the bed, you have to climb down to the foot of it in order to find a patch of floor space to stand on. Outside, I am within a few yards of a liquor store, a bar that advertises "free beer tomorrow," a convenience store, and a Burger King—but no supermarket or, alas, laundromat. By reputation, the Overseas park is a nest of crime and crack, and I am hoping at least for some vibrant, multicultural street life. But desolation rules night and day, except for a thin stream of pedestrian traffic heading for their jobs at the Sheraton or 7-Eleven. There are not exactly people here but what amounts to canned labor, being preserved from the heat between shifts.

In line with my reduced living conditions, a new form of ugliness arises at Jerry's. First we are confronted—via an announcement on the computers through which we input orders—with the new rule that the hotel bar is henceforth off-limits to restaurant employees. The culprit, I learn through the grapevine, is the ultra-efficient gal who trained me—another trailer-home dweller and a mother of three. Something had set her off one morning, so she slipped out for a nip and returned to the floor impaired. This mostly hurts Ellen, whose habit it is to free her hair from its rubber band and drop by the bar for a couple of Zins before heading home at the end of the shift, but all of us feel the chill. Then the next day, when I go for straws, for the first time I find the dry-storage room locked. Ted, the portly assistant manager who opens it for me, explains that he caught one of the dishwashers attempting to steal something, and, unfortunately, the miscreant will be with us until a replacement can be found—hence the locked door. I neglect to ask what he had been trying to steal, but Ted tells me who he is—the kid with the buzz cut and the earring [George].

* * *

When my month-long plunge into poverty is almost over, I finally land my dream job—housekeeping. I do this by walking into the personnel office of the only place I figure I might have some credibility, the hotel attached to Jerry's, and confiding urgently that I have to have a second job if I am to pay my rent and, no, it couldn't be front-desk clerk. "All right," the personnel lady fairly spits, "So it's housekeeping," and she marches me back to meet Maria, the housekeeping manager, a tiny, frenetic Hispanic woman who greets me as "babe" and hands me a pamphlet emphasizing the need for a positive attitude. The hours are nine in the morning till whenever, the pay is $6.10 an hour, and there's one week of vacation a year. I don't have to ask about health insurance once I meet Carlotta, the middle-aged African-American woman who will be training me. Carla, as she tells me to call her, is missing all of her top front teeth.

On that first day of housekeeping and last day of my entire project—although I don't yet know it's the last—Carla is in a foul mood. We have been given nineteen rooms to clean, most of them "checkouts," as opposed to "stay-overs," that require the whole enchilada of bed-stripping, vacuuming, and bathroom-scrubbing. When one of the rooms that had been listed as a stay-over turns out to be a checkout, Carla calls Maria to complain, but of course to no avail. "So make up the motherfucker," Carla orders me, and I do the beds while she sloshes around the bathroom. For four hours without a break I strip and remake beds, taking about four and a half minutes per queen-sized bed, which I could get down to three if there were any reason to. We try to avoid vacuuming by picking up the larger specks by hand, but often there is nothing to do but drag the monstrous vacuum cleaner—it weighs about thirty pounds—off our cart and try to wrestle it around the floor. Sometimes Carla hands me the squirt bottle of "BAM" (an acronym for something that begins, ominously, with "butyric"; the rest has been worn off the label) and lets me do the bathrooms. No service ethic challenges me here to new heights of performance. I just concentrate on removing the pubic hairs from the bathtubs, or at least the dark ones that I can see.

I had looked forward to the breaking-and-entering aspect of cleaning the stay-overs, the chance to examine the secret, physical existence of strangers. But the contents of the rooms are always banal and surprisingly neat—zipped up shaving kits, shoes lined up against the wall (there are no closets), flyers for snorkeling trips, maybe an empty wine bottle or two. It is the TV that keeps us going, from *Jerry* to *Sally* to *Hawaii Five-O* and then on to the soaps. If there's something especially arresting, like "Won't Take No for an Answer" on *Jerry,* we sit down on the edge of a bed and giggle for a moment as if this were a pajama party instead of a terminally dead-end job. The soaps are the best, and Carla turns the volume up full blast so that she won't miss anything from the bathroom or while the vacuum is on. In room 503, Marcia confronts Jeff about Lauren. In 505, Lauren taunts poor cuckolded Marcia. In 511, Helen offers Amanda $10,000 to stop seeing Eric, prompting Carla to emerge from the bathroom to study Amanda's troubled face. "You take it, girl," she advises. "I would for sure."

The tourists' rooms that we clean and, beyond them, the far more expensively appointed interiors in the soaps, begin after a while to merge. We have entered a better world—a world of comfort where every day is a day off, waiting to be filled up with sexual intrigue. We, however, are only gate-crashers in this fantasy, forced to pay for our presence with backaches and perpetual thirst. The mirrors, and there are far too many of them in hotel rooms, contain the kind of person you would normally find pushing a shopping cart down a city street—bedraggled, dressed in a damp hotel polo shirt two sizes too large, and with sweat dribbling down her chin like drool. I am enormously relieved when Carla announces a half-hour meal break, but my appetite fades when I see that the bag of hot-dog rolls she has been carrying around on our cart is not trash salvaged from a checkout but what she has brought for her lunch.

When I request permission to leave at about 3:30, another housekeeper warns me that no one has so far succeeded in combining housekeeping at the hotel with serving at Jerry's: "Some kid did it once for five days, and you're no kid." With that helpful information in mind, I rush back to number 46, down four Advils (the name brand this time), shower, stooping to fit into the stall, and attempt to compose myself for the oncoming shift. So much for what Marx termed the "reproduction of labor power," meaning the things a worker has to do just so she'll be ready to work again. The only unforeseen obstacle to the smooth transition from job to job is that my tan Jerry's slacks, which had looked reasonably clean by 40-watt bulb last night when I hand-washed my Hawaiian shirt, prove by daylight to be mottled with ketchup and ranch-dressing stains. I spend most of my hour-long break between jobs attempting to remove the edible portions with a sponge and then drying the slacks over the hood of my car in the sun.

I can do this two-job thing, is my theory, if I can drink enough caffeine and avoid getting distracted by George's ever more obvious suffering.[7]

* * *

I resolve to give him all my tips that night and to hell with the experiment in low-wage money management. At eight, Ellen and I grab a snack together standing at the mephitic end of the kitchen counter, but I can only manage two or three mozzarella sticks and lunch had been a mere handful of McNuggets. I am not tired at all, I assure myself, though it may be that there is simply no more "I" left to do the tiredness monitoring. What I would see, if I were more alert to the situation, is that the forces of destruction are already massing against me. There is only one cook on duty, a young man named Jesus ("Hay-Sue," that is) and he is new to the job. And there is Joy, who shows up to take over in the middle of the shift, wearing high heels and a long, clingy white dress and fuming as if she'd just been stood up in some cocktail bar.

Then it comes, the perfect storm. Four of my tables fill up at once. Four tables is nothing for me now, but only so long as they are obligingly staggered. As I bev table 27, tables 25, 28, and 24 are watching enviously. As I bev 25, 24 glowers because their bevs haven't even been ordered. Twenty-eight is four yuppyish types, meaning everything on the side and agonizing instructions as to the chicken Caesars. Twenty-five is a middle-aged black couple, who complain, with some justice, that the iced tea isn't fresh and the tabletop is sticky. But table 24 is the meteorological event of the century:

---

[7] In 1996, the number of persons holding two or more jobs averaged 7.8 million, or 6.2 percent of the workforce. It was about the same rate for men and for women (6.1 versus 6.2), though the kinds of jobs differ by gender. About two thirds of multiple jobholders work one job full-time and the other part-time. Only a heroic minority—4 percent of men and 2 percent of women—work two full-time jobs simultaneously. (From John F. Stinson Jr., "New Data on Multiple Jobholding Available from the CPS," in the *Monthly Labor Review*, March 1997.)

ten British tourists who seem to have made the decision to absorb the American experience entirely by mouth. Here everyone has at least two drinks—iced tea and milk shake, Michelob and water (with lemon slice, please)—and a huge promiscuous orgy of breakfast specials, mozz sticks, chicken strips, quesadillas, burgers with cheese and without, sides of hash browns with cheddar, with onions, with gravy, seasoned fries, plain fries, banana splits. Poor Jesus! Poor me! Because when I arrive with their first tray of food—after three prior trips just to refill bevs—Princess Di refuses to eat her chicken strips with her pancake-and-sausage special, since, as she now reveals, the strips were meant to be an appetizer. Maybe the others would have accepted their meals, but Di, who is deep into her third Michelob, insists that everything else go back while they work on their "starters." Meanwhile, the yuppies are waving me down for more decaf and the black couple looks ready to summon the NAACP.

Much of what happened next is lost in the fog of war. Jesus starts going under. The little printer on the counter in front of him is spewing out orders faster than he can rip them off, much less produce the meals. Even the invincible Ellen is ashen from stress. I bring table 24 their reheated main courses, which they immediately reject as either too cold or fossilized by the microwave. When I return to the kitchen with their trays (three trays in three trips), Joy confronts me with arms akimbo: "What is this?" She means the food—the plates of rejected pancakes, hash browns in assorted flavors, toasts, burgers, sausages, eggs. "Uh, scrambled with cheddar," I try, "and that's . . ." "NO," she screams in my face. "Is it a traditional, a super-scramble, an eye-opener?" I pretend to study my check for a clue, but entropy has been up to its tricks, not only on the plates but in my head, and I have to admit that the original order is beyond reconstruction. "You don't know an eye-opener from a traditional?" she demands in outrage. All I know, in fact, is that my legs have lost interest in the current venture and have announced their intention to fold. I am saved by a yuppie (mercifully not one of mine) who chooses this moment to charge into the kitchen to bellow that his food is twenty-five minutes late. Joy screams at him to get the hell out of her kitchen, please, and then turns on Jesus in a fury, hurling an empty tray across the room for emphasis.

I leave. I don't walk out, I just leave. I don't finish my side work or pick up my credit-card tips, if any, at the cash register or, of course, ask Joy's permission to go. And the surprising thing is that you can walk out without permission, that the door opens, that the thick tropical night air parts to let me pass, that my car is still parked where I left it. There is no vindication in this exit, no fuck-you surge of relief, just an overwhelming, dank sense of failure pressing down on me and the entire parking lot. I had gone into this venture in the spirit of science, to test a mathematical proposition, but somewhere along the line, in the tunnel vision imposed by long shifts and relentless concentration, it became a test of myself, and clearly I have failed. Not only had I flamed out as a housekeeper/server, I had even forgotten to give George my tips, and, for reasons perhaps best known to hardworking, generous people like Gail and Ellen, this hurts. I don't cry, but I am in a position to realize, for the first time in many years, that the tear ducts are still there, and still capable of doing their job.

When I moved out of the trailer park, I gave the key to number 46 to Gail and arranged for my deposit to be transferred to her. She told me that Joan is still living in her van and that Stu had been fired from the Hearthside. I never found out what happened to George.

In one month, I had earned approximately $1,040 and spent $517 on food, gas, toiletries, laundry, phone, and utilities. If I had remained in my $500 efficiency, I would have been able to pay the rent and have $22 left over (which is $78 less than the cash I had in my pocket at the start of the month). During this time I bought no clothing except for the required slacks and no prescription drugs or medical care (I did finally buy some vitamin B to compensate for the lack of vegetables in my diet). Perhaps I could have saved a little on food if I had gotten to a supermarket more often, instead of convenience stores, but it should be noted that I lost almost four pounds in four weeks, on a diet weighted heavily toward burgers and fries.

How former welfare recipients and single mothers will (and do) survive in the low-wage workforce, I cannot imagine. Maybe they will figure out how to condense their lives—including child-raising, laundry, romance, and meals—into the couple of hours between full-time jobs. Maybe they will take up residence in their vehicles, if they have one. All I know is that I couldn't hold two jobs and I couldn't make enough money to live on with one. And I had advantages unthinkable to many of the long-term poor—health, stamina, a working car, and no children to care for and support. Certainly nothing in my experience contradicts the conclusion of Kathryn Edin and Laura Lein, in their recent book *Making Ends Meet: How Single Mothers Survive Welfare and Low-Wage Work*, that low-wage work actually involves more hardship and deprivation than life at the mercy of the welfare state. In the coming months and years, economic conditions for the working poor are bound to worsen, even without the almost inevitable recession. As mentioned earlier, the influx of former welfare recipients into the low-skilled workforce will have a depressing effect on both wages and the number of jobs available. A general economic downturn will only enhance these effects, and the working poor will of course be facing it without the slight, but nonetheless often saving, protection of welfare as a backup.

The thinking behind welfare reform was that even the humblest jobs are morally uplifting and psychologically buoying. In reality they are likely to be fraught with insult and stress. But I did discover one redeeming feature of the most abject low-wage work—the camaraderie of people who are, in almost all cases, far too smart and funny and caring for the work they do and the wages they're paid. The hope, of course, is that someday these people will come to know what they're worth, and take appropriate action.

STUDY QUESTIONS

1. Why was it easy for the author to talk with her co-workers about their living situations?

2. After two weeks of work, what did the author realize?

3. The Federal Poverty line is revised every year, but is roughly $11,000 per year for an individual. Create a monthly budget for living off this amount (be realistic as possible), and discuss your findings.

4. Visit Ehrenreich's website, www.barbaraehrenreich.com, and read her recent discussion of the implications of her work in today's economic climate. How is the **economy** getting more challenging for low-income families?

RILEY E. DUNLAP

The Evolution of Environmental Sociology: A Brief History and Assessment of the American Experience

E nvironmental problems—especially those caused by human behavior—seem to have been present throughout human history, but these problems are now more pervasive, and on a larger scale, than ever. According to Riley E. Dunlap, a key founder in the field of **environmental sociology**, as the nature of these environmental problems have changed in recent decades, so have **society** and **sociology**'s stances toward them. Dunlap traces the history of environmental sociology, concluding that the larger field of sociology has come a long way in its views about the **environment**, but it has farther to go.

NEARLY TWO DECADES AGO CATTON* AND I TRIED TO CODIFY THE burgeoning but diverse body of sociological work on environmental issues being conducted primarily but not exclusively in the United States by providing an explicit definition of the field of environmental sociology. Included in a thematic issue of *The American Sociologist* devoted to "New Theoretical Perspectives in Sociology," our article defined the field as "the study of interaction between the environment and society" (Catton and Dunlap, 1978). We also contended that examining such interaction would

Handbook of Environmental Sociology by Dunlap, Riley E.; Michelson, William. Reproduced with permission of GREENWOOD PUBLISHING GROUP, INCORPORATED in the format republished in a book via Copyright Clearance Center.

---

* Sociologist William R. Catton Jr. (b. 1926), a frequent collaborator of the author's.

require overcoming sociology's traditional and deep-seated reluctance to acknowledge the relevance of the physical environment for understanding contemporary societies.

We argued that in particular the Durkheimian* tradition of explaining social phenomena only in terms of other "social facts," plus an aversion to earlier excesses of biological and geographical "determinism," had led sociologists to ignore the physical world in which humans live. These disciplinary traditions were further strengthened, we suggested, by the emergence of sociology during an era of unprecedented growth and prosperity, fuelled by resource abundance and technological progress. Along with increased urbanization, which reduced contact with nature, these societal trends made it easy for sociologists to assume that, at least within industrial societies, human life was becoming increasingly independent of the physical world. Consequently, we claimed that our discipline had come to assume that the exceptional features of homo sapiens—language, technology, science and culture more generally—made industrialized societies "exempt" from the constraints of nature. We concluded by claiming that changing circumstances (such as the 1973–4 energy crisis) necessitated shedding the "blinkers" imposed by exemptionalism and adopting an ecological paradigm or world view that acknowledges the ecosystem-dependence of all human societies.[1]

It is clear, in retrospect, that our call for a paradigmatic revolution was issued during an exuberant period for the new field of environmental sociology. It had been formally recognized via establishment of a "Section" within the American Sociological Association (ASA) in 1976, following similar developments in the Rural Sociological Society (RSS) and the Society for the Study of Social Problems (SSSP) (Dunlap and Catton, 1979). Buttel (1987: 466) has described this period as one in which "there was a vibrant *esprit de corps* that a new sociology was being nurtured.... Environmental sociologists sought nothing less than the reorientation of sociology toward a more holistic perspective that would conceptualise social processes within the context of the biosphere." Writing a decade ago, Buttel (ibid.) went on to argue, "These lofty intentions ... have largely failed to come to fruition. The discipline at large has handily withstood the challenges to its theoretical assumptions posed by environmental sociologists." While not challenging the accuracy of Buttel's appraisal of the situation at that time, I believe his pessimistic assessment of environmental sociology and his apparent confidence in the continuing hegemony of exemptionalist thinking within the larger discipline were heavily influenced by the period in which he was writing. The late 1970s were indeed a "vibrant" period for environmental sociology, but the 1980s saw a significant decline of interest in the field, reaching its nadir at mid-decade, when Buttel wrote his overview. Since the late 1980s there has been a resurgence of interest in environmental sociology within the USA and internationally, and the larger discipline's misplaced faith in

---

* Relating to French sociologist Emile Durkheim (1858–1917).

human exemptionalism has been increasingly called into question by environmental sociologists as well as by societal developments.

* * *

THE CHANGING NATURE OF ENVIRONMENTAL PROBLEMS

The growing salience of environmental problems over the past decade stemmed, not only from increased attention to them by scientists, media and policy makers, but from discernible changes in the nature of the problems. Contemporary environmental problems differ from earlier ones such as litter, loss of natural areas and air and water pollution in a number of critical respects. First, the scale of such problems has increased from typically localized problems (such as urban air pollution and pollution of rivers) to the regional level (as with acid rain) and even global level (for example, ozone depletion), thereby potentially affecting far more people. Second, localized problems such as contaminated water supplies and inadequate solid waste repositories occur (and are reported in the media) with enough frequency for them to be seen as generalized problems, adding to the sense that environmental deterioration is pervasive. Third, environmental problems are increasingly recognized as often having origins that are poorly understood and consequences that are difficult to detect and predict, with the result that they appear "riskier" than earlier predecessors (Ungar, 1995). Fourth, the impacts of many problems pose serious consequences for the health and welfare of humans (including future generations) as well as for other species, and some of these impacts may be irreversible. In short, environmental problems appear to have increased in frequency, scale and seriousness (Dunlap, 1993). Whereas in the 1960s and early 1970s environmental degradation often seemed an aesthetic issue (or, at most, an irritant affecting outdoor activities), it is increasingly seen as a direct threat to human health and well-being, from the local level (for example, toxic wastes) to the global level (for example, ozone depletion).

To summarize, the past decade has seen the emergence of widespread societal recognition of the fact that human activities are causing a deterioration in the quality of the environment, *and* that environmental deterioration in turn has negative impacts on people (Dunlap and Mertig, 1992). Thus the fundamental subject matter of environmental sociology—the relationship between humans and the environment—is much more obvious and seen as far more significant than when Buttel wrote his pessimistic appraisal of the field in the mid-1980s or even when the field was emerging in the 1970s. In addition, growing recognition of the health threat posed by many environmental conditions makes it apparent that not only do human–environment interactions occur at the symbolic or cognitive level, once posited as the core of environmental sociology (Klausner, 1971), but that such conditions can have direct (and deleterious) impacts on human behaviour and well-being.

Especially significant have been the gradual development of scientific consensus and widespread public concern over the reality of human-induced global environmental change such as ozone depletion, loss of biodiversity and, to a lesser extent, global climate change (Dunlap, 1996). The finite ability of ecosystems to absorb the by-products of industrialization without disruption is increasingly seen as a more pressing limit than is scarcity of natural resources. Global environmental change highlights the fact that ecosystems serve not only as "resource depot" and "waste repository" for human societies, but as our "living space" as well, and that these three uses are increasingly in conflict (Dunlap, 1993). For example, ozone depletion and global warming—both the result of the global ecosystem's inability to absorb industrial pollutants without being altered—may affect where humans can live safely as well as the availability of agricultural crops and other resources. Ultimately, ecological limits on humans stem from the finite ability of ecosystems (from local to global) to fulfil these three increasingly competing functions.

Widespread recognition of the human origins and consequences of global environmental change (GEC) represents an enormous opportunity for environmental sociology, as well as an obvious anomaly for human exemptionalism. Examining the human dimensions of GEC necessitates study of society–environment interactions, including a balanced examination of the impacts of humans on the environment as well as the effects of ecological constraints on human societies (Stern, 1993). Further, the range of potential societal responses to such change (denial, adaptation, mitigation and so on) highlights the vital role of human agency in responding to ecological constraints. In fact, we must acknowledge that our original call for the abandonment of the exemptionalist paradigm tended to emphasize the importance of ecological constraints and to play down the potential of modern reflexive societies to cope with (but not escape) such constraints (Spaargaren and Mol, 1992).

REVITALIZATION OF ENVIRONMENTAL SOCIOLOGY

Given the dramatic increase in the societal salience of environmental issues—measured by environmental activism, media attention, public opinion and policy making—in the USA since the late 1980s, it is not surprising that sociological interest in these topics was also rekindled. This is apparent from a variety of indicators, including membership in the ASA Section on Environment and Technology. After bottoming out from 1983 to 1985 and increasing only slightly over the next three years, section membership grew rapidly in the late 1980s and early 1990s, reaching its peak in 1993 and levelling off to around 400 since then. The field's revitalization is also confirmed by the publication of several new texts (Cable and Cable, 1995; Cylke, 1993; Foster, 1994; Harper, 1996; Schnaiberg and Gould, 1994), an obvious indicator of growing interest among both faculty and students. Finally, the few departments offering formal graduate training in the field have experienced a sharp increase in student interest.

Most significantly, unlike the situation in the 1970s, environmental sociology is now receiving a good deal of attention internationally, as evidenced by this volume. Indeed, in the 1990s a majority of the potential texts written in English have been written by Canadians (Hannigan, 1995; Mehta and Ouellet, 1995; Murphy, 1994) and Europeans (Dickens, 1992; 1996; Goldblatt, 1996; Martell, 1994; Yearley, 1991). Recent years have also seen the formation of environmental sociology organizations in countries such as the UK and Japan, and the formation of 'environmental social science associations' in Scandinavia, Brazil and Canada. In addition, a Working Group on Environment and Society, launched within the International Sociological Association in 1990, grew rapidly and achieved research committee status in record time.[2] In short, in the 1990s environmental sociology is being institutionalized internationally along the same lines as occurred in the USA in the 1970s. This likely reflects, in part, the fact that environmental conditions are now viewed as problematic in virtually all nations, as well as being inherently global in nature (Dunlap *et al.*, 1993).

Much of this new and renewed interest in environmental issues, both in the USA and elsewhere, has taken the form of sociological analyses of societal reaction to environmental problems in the form of studies of public opinion and perceptions, environmentalism, green politics and environmental policy making (see, for example, Hannigan, 1995; Martell, 1994; Yearley, 1991). The political economy of environmental problems and sociological contributions to risk analyses, both discerned as emerging areas by Buttel (1987), have continued to attract increasing attention. While some traditional sub-areas such as housing and the built environment and social impact assessment have apparently not yet benefited much from the revitalization of sociological interest in the environment (perhaps because they are only indirectly affected by the upturn in societal interest in environmental problems), new research emphases have emerged. Most obvious in the USA has been the virtual explosion of interest in issues related to growing awareness of the pervasiveness of environmental hazards at the local level: studies of community reaction to local hazards; the rapidly spreading NIMBY ("Not In My Back Yard") syndrome; the emergence of local, grassroots environmental groups; and the interrelated phenomena of "environmental racism" (the location of hazards in predominantly minority areas) and the emerging "environmental justice" movement among minorities.[3]

In addition to the wide range of work noted above, the revitalization of environmental sociology is particularly apparent from a recent spate of publications self-consciously designed as contributions to the methodological, conceptual and theoretical "core" of the field—something that was notably absent during the 1980s. Many of these contributions involve efforts to apply insights from traditional theoretical perspectives, ranging from symbolic interactionism to Marxism, to help understand human–environment relations, yet their authors (who are often British) frequently acknowledge the limitations imposed by the "exemptionalist" nature of these perspectives and call for a reorientation away from our traditional disciplinary assumption that the biophysical environment is irrelevant to modern, industrialized societies (Benton, 1991; Dickens, 1992, 1996; Goldblatt, 1996; Jones, 1990; Murphy, 1994; Weigert, 1991). In addition to these efforts at "greening"* sociological theory, renewed attention is also being paid to conceptual and methodological issues involved in examining society–environment interactions, primarily by empirically oriented American scholars (Freudenburg and Gramling, 1993; Gramling and Freudenburg, 1996; Freudenburg *et al.*, 1995; Kroll-Smith and Couch, 1991; Kroll-Smith *et al.*, 1996). The eventual merging of these theoretical and empirical efforts promises to yield important advances in understanding the nature of society–environment relations.

In sum, although most of the 1980s, the so-called "Decade of Greed," was a difficult time for environmental sociology in the USA, recent years have seen a dramatic resurgence of interest in the field and signs of its intellectual revitalization. Despite Reagan†-era efforts to define environmental conditions as non-problematic, they continued to worsen and their significant impacts on humans became increasingly apparent. In other words, real-world conditions (and, of course, societal attention to them) seem to have stimulated renewed sociological attention to the environment (see, for example, Foster, 1994: 8).

* * *

CONCLUDING OBSERVATIONS

I conclude by assessing the current standing of sociological interest in environmental issues relative to Catton's and my original call for the development of environmental sociology as a distinct area of specialization and for adoption of an ecological paradigm to guide it. In terms of the former, it is obvious that, despite some ups and downs, environmental sociology has established itself as a viable area of specialization, not only in the USA but throughout much of the world. Indeed, it has become institutionalized at the international level. Moreover, at least in Europe, environmental issues have

---

* Green is often associated with environmentalism, so greening means to make something more positive environmentally.

† Ronald Reagan (1911–2004), fortieth president of the United States.

begun to receive considerable attention and are increasingly assigned theoretical import in the larger discipline. Overall, our hope for increased sociological attention to the environment has been exceeded.

Our plea for replacing the discipline's human exemptionalism paradigm with an ecological one is more difficult to assess, in part because it was inherently more ambiguous as well as provocative. One's assessment clearly depends upon one's interpretation of our call for a paradigmatic shift, which in turn is heavily influenced by one's conception of "paradigm."

* * *

In conclusion, while it has a long way to go, I think sociology has made considerable progress towards recognizing the importance of the ecological dimension of human existence during the past two decades. If the trend continues, I suspect that analyses of ecological matters—both empirical and theoretical—may eventually become so common among sociologists that there will no longer be a need for an "environmental sociology" per se. This would represent the ultimate demise of human exemptionalism in our discipline.

NOTES

1. We originally labelled the dominant disciplinary perspective the "human *exceptionalist* paradigm," but subsequently shifted to the "human *exemptionalist* paradigm" to acknowledge that we were not questioning that homo sapiens possessed 'exceptional' characteristics, but only that these characteristics "exempted" our species from ecological constraints. Likewise, we revised the call for a "new *environmental* paradigm" to that for a "new *ecological* paradigm" (Dunlap and Catton, 1979; Catton and Dunlap, 1980). For an update of the HEP-NEP argument, see Dunlap and Catton (1994).
2. This was accomplished by a merger with the existing Research Committee on Social Ecology.
3. See, for example, the special issue of *Social Problems* (February 1993) devoted to "environmental justice," the special issue of *Sociological Spectrum* (January–March 1993) devoted to "New Directions in Hazard, Risk and Disaster Research" and the special issue of *Sociological Perspectives* (Summer 1996) devoted to "Environmental Conflicts."

REFERENCES

Benton, Ted (1991), "Biology and Social Science: Why the Return of the Repressed Should Be Given A (Cautious) Welcome," *Sociology*, 25, 1–29.

Buttel, Frederick H. (1987). "New Directions in Environmental Sociology," *Annual Review of Sociology*, 13, 465–88.

Cable, Sherry and Charles Cable (1995), *Environmental Problems/Grassroots Solutions,* New York: St Martin's Press.

Catton, William R. and Riley E. Dunlap (1978), "Environmental Sociology: A New Paradigm," *The American Sociologist*, 13, 41–9.

Catton, William R. and Riley E. Dunlap (1980). "A New Ecological Paradigm for Post-Exuberant Sociology," *American Behavioral Scientist*, 24, 15–47.

Cylke, F. Kurt (1993), *The Environment*, New York: Harper Collins.

Dickens, Peter (1992), *Society and Nature: Towards a Green Social Theory*, Philadelphia: Temple University Press.

Dickens, Peter (1996), *Reconstructing Nature: Alienation, Emancipation and the Division of Labour*, London/New York: Routledge.

Dunlap, Riley E. (1993), "From Environmental to Ecological Problems," in C. Calhoun and G. Ritzer (eds), *Social Problems*, New York: McGraw-Hill; reprinted in M. Redclift and G. Woodgate (eds), *The Sociology of the Environment*, Vol. 1, Aldershot/Brookfield: Edward Elgar, 1995.

Dunlap, Riley E. (1996), "Public Perceptions of Global Warming: A Cross-National Comparison," in Human Dimensions of Global Environmental Change Program (ed.), *Global Change, Local Challenge*, Vol. 2. Geneva: Human Dimensions Program.

Dunlap, Riley E. and William R. Catton (1979), "Environmental Sociology," *Annual Review of Sociology*, 5, 243–73.

Dunlap, Riley E. and William R. Catton (1994), "Toward an Ecological Sociology: The Development, Current Status and Probable Future of Environmental Sociology," in W.V. D'Antonio, M. Sasaki and Y. Yonebayashi (eds), *Ecology, Society & The Quality of Social Life*, New Brunswick/London: Transaction Publishers.

Dunlap, Riley E. and Angela G. Mertig (eds) (1992), *American Environmentalism: The U.S. Environmental Movement, 1970–1990*. Washington, DC: Taylor and Francis.

Dunlap, Riley E., George H. Gallup and Alec M. Gallup (1993), "Of Global Concern: Results of the Health of the Planet Survey," *Environment*, 35, November, 6–15, 33–9.

Foster, John Bellamy (1994). *The Vulnerable Planet*, New York: Monthly Review Press.

Freudenburg, William R. and Robert Gramling (1993), "Socioenvironmental Factors and Development Policy: Understanding Opposition and Support for Offshore Oil Development," *Sociological Forum*, 8, 341–64.

Freudenburg, William R., Scott Frickel and Robert Gramling (1995), "Beyond the Nature/Society Divide: Learning to Think About a Mountain," *Sociological Forum*, 10, 361–92.

Goldblatt, David (1996), *Social Theory and the Environment*, Boulder, CO: Westview.

Gramling, Robert and William R. Freudenburg (1996), "Environmental Sociology: Toward a Paradigm for the 21st Century," *Sociological Spectrum*, 16, 47–60.

Hannigan, John A. (1995), *Environmental Sociology: A Social Constructionist Perspective*, London/New York: Routledge.

Harper, Charles L. (1996), *Environment and Society*, Upper Saddle River: Prentice-Hall.

Jones, Alwyn (1990), "Social Symbiosis: A Gaian Critique of Contemporary Social Theory," *The Ecologist*, 20, 108–13.

Klausner, Samuel Z. (1971). *On Man in His Environment*, San Francisco: Jossey-Bass.

Kroll-Smith, J. Stephen and Stephen R. Couch (1991), "What is a Disaster? An Ecological–Symbolic Approach to Resolving the Definitional Debate," *International Journal of Mass Emergencies and Disasters*, 9, 355–66.

Kroll-Smith, Steve, Valerie Gunter and Shirley Laska (1996), "The Symbolic, the Physical and Sociology: How We Theorize Environments," paper presented at the Annual Meeting of the American Sociological Association, New York, August.

Martell, Luke (1994), *Environment and Society*, Amherst: University of Massachusetts Press.

Mehta, Michael D. and Eric Ouellet (eds) (1995), *Environmental Sociology: Theory and Practice*, North York: Captus Press.

Murphy, Raymond (1994), *Rationality & Nature*, Boulder, CO: Westview.

Schnaiberg, Allan and Kenneth Alan Gould (1994), *Environment and Society: The Enduring Conflict*, New York: St. Martin's Press.

Spaargaren, Gert and Arthur P.J. Mol (1992), "Sociology, Environment and Modernity: Ecological Modernization as a Theory of Social Change," *Society and Natural Resource*, 5, 323–44.

Stern, Paul C. (1993), "A Second Environmental Science: Human-Environment Interactions," *Science*, 260, 1897–9.

Ungar, Sheldon (1995), "Social Scares and Global Warming: Beyond the Rio Convention," *Society and Natural Resources*, 8, 443–56.

Weigert, Andrew J. (1991), "Transverse Interaction: A Pragmatic Perspective on Environment as Other," *Symbolic Interaction*, 14, 353–63.

Yearley, Steven (1991), *The Green Case: A Sociology of Environmental Issues, Arguments and Politics*, London: Harper-Collins.

STUDY QUESTIONS

1. Identify at least two ways that contemporary **environmental** problems differ from earlier environmental problems, according to Dunlap.

2. How does Dunlap feel about the ability of **environmental sociology** to tackle current and future environmental problems?

3. To what does the author attribute the revitalization of environmental sociology after the 1980s?

4. Dunlap discusses both how humans affect the environment and how those changes in turn affect human **societies**. Name at least three unexpected ways in which environmental change that we caused now affects us.

Index